SCRAPPING THE SOUTHERN

THE DISPOSAL OF SOUTHERN REGION STEAM

Jeffery Grayer

NOODLE BOOKS

© Jeffery Grayer and Noodle Books 2013

ISBN 978-1-906419-70-7

First published in 2013 by Kevin Robertson
under the **NOODLE BOOKS** imprint
PO Box 279
Corhampton
SOUTHAMPTON
SO32 3ZX

www.noodlebooks.co.uk

Printed in England by Berforts Information Press Ltd. Oxford.

Front cover - *Last of the Bulleids to be cut up at Newport was No 34017 "Ilfracombe" which spent some months in Buttigieg's yard before final despatch in December 1968. (JG)*

Frontispiece - *Masquerading as "Guildford" this is in fact No 30921 "Shrewsbury" seen in the pastoral surroundings of Cohen's scrapyard near Kettering. LT Underground stock completes this bizarre scene. (JG)*

Opposite - *Death of a King. N15 class 4-6-0 No. 30453 "King Arthur" himself awaiting the cutter's torch at an Eastleigh Works open day in 1961. No. 30453 had been considered for preservation, but there were others of the class thought to be in better condition and in the event it was decided that an example with an Ashford style cab, No 30777, would have better route availability and "King Arthur" was scrapped in October 1961 without ceremony. Note the style of dress of the schoolboy enthusiasts of the time complete with attaché cases, satchels and school blazers. (Barry Lewis)*

Rear cover - *No 35008 "Orient Line" in company with assorted ex GWR items awaits its turn in Buttigieg's yard Newport on 21 April 1968. Bulleid pacifics present at other Newport yards on this date were Nos 34024, 34060, 34089, 34098, 34108, 34104, 34047, 34008, 34102, 35030 and 34017. (Jonathan Martin)*

All uncredited views have been sourced from unknown collections with no annotation as to ownership / copyright indicated.

CONTENTS

1. Introduction

Scrapping locomotives is nothing new, it has been going on since railways were invented as technological progress rendered previous designs redundant. In this volume we examine the history of scrapping since the grouping on the Southern Railway, later the Southern Region of British Railways, through to the end of steam on the region in July 1967 and on to 1968 when the last locomotives were towed away from their storage sites to the scrapyard.

We look at the in-house scrapping which took place at the various Railway Works inherited from the pre-Grouping companies and the eventual outsourcing to private scrapyards from 1964 onwards brought on by the sheer volume of material awaiting disposal. Inherently a depressing subject to steam lovers, there is however something morbidly fascinating about the views contained herein. Scenes of rusting, dismembered locomotives, often set against a contrasting background of lush vegetation combine to produce powerful emotive images.

I am grateful to the various photographic contributors to this book who have allowed me access to their work. I am particularly appreciative of the co-operation of Eric Best, a former BR employee involved in the scrapping process at Eastleigh Works from 1958 – 1963, who not only provided some fascinating images of the gang at work but also some vivid recollections of what the job was actually like.

I well remember visiting Woodham's scrapyard at Barry for the first time in the mid 1960's and the lasting impression that walking up and down row upon row of silent former giants of the steam age left with me. I also recall wandering around the scrap lines at Eastleigh Shed where the locomotives awaited the final brief trip round to the back of the Works where the scrapping took place. Finally, visits to the dumping grounds at Weymouth and Salisbury sheds in 1967/68 brought home that this really was the end of an era.

Much of the published information concerning the history of locomotive disposals has previously come from the booklets produced by Peter Hands entitled *"What Happened to Steam"*. It has been apparent for some time that much of this information is inaccurate and a project is currently underway to attempt to address this. Entitled *"What Really Happened to Steam"*, details of this venture can be found at the website www.whatreallyhappenedtosteam.co.uk. It is the intention to eventually publish as definitive an account as is possible, more than five decades after the events, detailing the documented end of the steam locomotives of all BR regions. In view of this it was thought prudent not to repeat previous errors by listing the fate of ex SR locomotives as gospel, such information must await their findings.

Jeffery Grayer 2013

No 34038 "Lynton", with rods removed, awaits the call to the scrapyard outside Eastleigh shed. This West Country pacific was withdrawn in June 1966 and was to be towed to Cashmore's scrapyard in Newport where it was despatched three months later. (JG)

2. Early Days & the Declining Fleet

The line-up at Kimbridge Sidings near Romsey in early 1948 with a fascinating array of antediluvian motive power evident.

We take up the story in the early years of the 20th. Century when, by 1905, Brighton Works was unable to keep pace with the number of locomotives requiring maintenance and backlogs began to build up. As a result the LB&SCR established concentrations of locomotives awaiting either entry to the works or scrapping at East Grinstead, Horsted Keynes and Horley. A review undertaken in 1908 by Robert Urie, in his capacity as Works Manager of Nine Elms Works found that 108 of the LB&SCR's 541 locomotives (20%) were either awaiting or under repair, and that a general overhaul at Brighton took 43 days, compared with just 7.2% of the locomotives of the SE&CR being currently under repair and only 21 days taken for a general overhaul being taken by Ashford Works. By 1910 the situation had deteriorated such that 30% of the LBSCR's locomotive stock was unusable due to delays and inefficiencies at Brighton Works.

Lawson Billinton, the District Locomotive Superintendent at New Cross Depot, had sought to alleviate the problems by executing repairs and boiler changes locally, but this had little impact on the overall problem. The LBSCR's Locomotive, Carriage and Wagon Superintendent Earle Marsh received much of the blame for the situation, which had been deteriorating for some years, and he was granted leave of absence due to sickness in 1910, followed by his resignation in July 1911. Billinton was invited to

take over on a temporary basis during Marsh's sickness, and promptly set about re-organising the Works and reducing the backlog by using the then emerging art of Time & Motion study techniques. In the 1870s William Stroudley had considered moving the locomotive Works to Horley but was persuaded to keep them in Brighton. Nevertheless, the sidings at Horley were used for storing withdrawn locomotives and those awaiting repair until the First World War. As late as March 1950 locomotives were still being scrapped at Horley wagon works when D1 No 2274 was despatched never having carried a BR number. Other locomotives believed to have been scrapped here include two O1 Class Nos 31123 and 31137.

The SR with its early electrification policies had allowed timely withdrawal of older classes such that the fleet passing into nationalised ownership in 1948 was already heavily pruned and in the next ten years only 392 locos from 40 classes were to be withdrawn.

By the end of 1947 Eastleigh was swamped with 65 derelict engines, so 27 were moved to the disused wartime loops at Kimbridge Junction near Romsey. The Railway Observer for February 1948 reported that, *"With no less than 53 withdrawn locomotives dumped, some having been out of service for 15 years, steps are being taken to reduce this store of*

5

SECR G class Nos 678 and an unknown Stirling 0-6-0 are seen in a parlous state at Ashford Works in this early view taken on 29 August 1925. Note the SE&CR plate still affixed to the cabside of the locomotive in the foreground. The five locomotives of what became the SECR G class had been ordered in 1898 by the GNoSR who were subsequently unable to pay for them. Consequently they were offered for sale by the builders, Messrs Neilson's, with the knowledge and authority of the GNoSR. Thus on 11 October 1899, Neilson's contacted the SE&CR, which had recently placed a locomotive order with them. The SECR was short of express passenger locomotives for the former LC&DR routes, which had a weight limit. The SECR quickly accepted the offer, paying £3,200 each, whereas Neilsons would have charged the GNoSR £2975 each. In December, the cost to the SECR was increased by a further £57 per engine and tender after Wainwright, the SECR Locomotive Superintendent, requested modifications including the fitting of vacuum brake equipment. On the SECR they were assigned as Class G, and entered service during January and February 1900, numbered 676–680. They passed to the SR at the Grouping, and, except for no. 678, were given SR numbers A676–A680. They were withdrawn from service between 1924 and 1927.

engines at Eastleigh by removing them in batches of 4 or 5 to sidings near Kimbridge Junction. Each batch is first checked over, oiled and all useful gauges, cab fittings etc. removed. Then the clanking procession is towed via Romsey, generally by an H15 but on one occasion by a Q1 piloting an N. It is understood that the w/d locos at Kimbridge Junc are destined for scrap in South Wales. On 16/2/48 a further batch of w/d locos was moved from Eastleigh Works to Baverstock sidings near Dinton including A12 613, 2 T1s, 4 and 364, and 3 D1s 2255, 2355 plus one other.

A later RO report stated that, "65 locos withdrawn at Eastleigh earlier this year are now being cut up either at the Works or at the ex RAF establishment at Dinton."

Others went from Eastleigh directly to Dinton where in the period 1948/9 some 50 life expired SR locos were cut up by contractors in Baverstock sidings. As mentioned in the Irwell Press book "Main Line to the West Part 2", "The resulting scrap metal was forwarded mainly to Barry, a significant location even at this early date, some larger components such as boilers being loaded onto bogie well wagons. It appears that some were sold on and used as stationary boilers in factories and market gardens.

Following this hundreds of old wagons arrived by special train or in formation of scheduled goods trains. The wagons were all labelled for the attention of a Mr Briggs. All iron and steel components including complete wheel sets were forwarded for scrap but some timber planking in good condition was sent away for further use. Timber in poor condition was used for firewood, coal being in short supply in austerity Britain."

The following locomotives are some of those known to have been scrapped at Dinton -

T1	4, 364
A12	555, 613, 614, 615, 618, 624, 630, 642, 643, 648, 652, 654
T3	571
X6	658, 666
K10	136, 138, 149, 342, 344, 381, 387, 388*
T14	445, 449, 460
D1	2255, 2259, 2355, 2699
I1X	2001, 2004, 2006, 2007, 2010, 2597, 2598, 2599, 2604
H1	2040

* see record page 9.

Dismantling in process at Dinton. The casual way asbestos coated boilers were dealt with is apparent. (J H Aston)

An undated view of the scrapline at Eastleigh with an eclectic mix including a saddle tank, LMS tender and Terriers. It would be interesting to know what might be lurking underneath those tarpaulins.

EARLY DAYS & THE DECLINING FLEET

T3 No. 563 stored at Kimbridge since 15 January 1948 and withdrawn back in August 1945 was reprieved and moved to Eastleigh for reconditioning and repainting to represent LSWR practice of earlier days at Waterloo in connection with the centenary celebrations in July. The locomotive was selected as it was the least altered from its original form of all locos stored there.

			BOILER			CYLINDERS		BLAST PIPE	LAGGING	CHARGE HAND	REMARKS
IN	OUT	TEN-DER	Num-ber	Pres-sure		Diameter L.	R.				
16⁴/40	7/8/40	205	1135	175	Chg	32 18⁵/8	32 18⁵/8	Rght.	Hood.	Jones Pate.	General.

§PS (11/46) **S.R.** Engine No. *388*   Class *K10 Mixed Traffic* (PS 833)

Engine Tender broken up Deviation WO 10200/47 at 17/4/48

Below - LSWR Jubilee Class 0-4-2 No 646 at Eastleigh, 10 June 1948. Built by Neilson and Co in 1893 and withdrawn 31 May 1939 but not cut up at Eastleigh until 1948, having been used as stationary boiler at Salisbury until December 1944. They were the last 0-4-2 tender engines in service in the UK.

Still displaying its Southern ownership, E4 0-6-2T (temporarily masquerading as an 0-4-0T) No 2518 was eventually withdrawn in 1955 and cut up at Ashford.

Some idea of the pace of withdrawals in the 1950s and 1960s can be gauged from the following figures compiled from Ian Allan ABC combined volumes

Year end loco totals excluding Standard classes:

BR locos in service year-end

1961	11691
1962	8767
1963	7050
1964	4973
1965	2987
1966	1689
1967	362
1968	3*

(* Vale of Rheidol narrow gauge)

Of these SR locos excluding Standards and Ivatt tanks totalled

1957	Summer	1444
1958	Summer	1211
1961	February	897
1962	July	617
1963	December	343
1964	July	224
1964	November	168
1966	January	100
1967	January	54
1967	July	30

Opposite top - Engine record card for No. 30197, broken up at Eastleigh.

Opposite bottom - Engine record card for No. 30579, sent to Brighton for scrap.

3. In-House Scrapping

It was a long-established tradition that Railway Companies constructed locomotives and scrapped them at their own works. Occasionally locomotives used on the SR were built by outside manufacturers, the main examples being Borsig of Berlin who built 10 examples of the L Class: Beyer-Peacock of Manchester who built a further 12: the USA tanks: the 700 Class built by Dübs of Glasgow: the L1s constructed by North British in Glasgow and a number of Ns built at the Woolwich Arsenal. However, scrapping was certainly reserved for the main works on the Southern Region i.e. Eastleigh for the LSWR, Brighton for the LBSCR and Ashford for the SE&CR. Brighton ceased scrapping activity in 1958 and the works closed in 1962. Ashford ceased scrapping in April 1962 although it continued to repair locomotives until June 1962, when all locomotive repairs moved to Eastleigh.

Eastleigh scrapped locomotives until 1964* when outsourcing was resorted to but continued to repair locomotives until No 34089 was outshopped on 3 October 1966, the event featuring on BBC News and Blue Peter. Considering steam traction was already condemned, investment in works repair at this late stage might appear somewhat strange but, it must be remembered that it been originally intended that the replacement electric traction for the Bournemouth line would take over from 1 January. For various reasons, mainly delivery of the new units, this was not possible and the changeover date was therefore pushed back further into 1967. The Southern motive-power department was now faced with a dilemma. The surviving steam engines were simply too run down to be able to maintain any sort of reliable service into 1967 so it was hurriedly agreed that certain repairs would be authorised. No 34089 was to benefit from this decision. From October 1966 all repairs would be concentrated at the various running sheds, meaning that, if an engine were now to develop a fault which in the past would have warranted a works visit, it would generally be condemned. (There were still some exceptions, but No 34089 would be the final recipient of an 'overhaul' for steam.)

* At least four steam locomotives were cut up outside the front of the running shed c1966 (see also list at Section 12). These included a Southern Mogul, Q1, BR Class 4 2-6-4T, and the locomotive - but not the tender - from No 35004 'Cunard White Star'. This last named engine was regarded as a 'good-un', had been through works in the summer of 1965 and was subsequently used on front-line passenger duties. Unfortunately shortly afterwards, a violent slip whilst working a train near Hook resulted in bent coupling and connecting rods. Even so this might not have been terminal, but for the associated breaking off of part of the tyre from the front nearside wheel. The engine was towed to Eastleigh and unceremoniously dumped outside the front of the shed whilst a decision was made regarding its future. When that came it was deemed unfit to move and was despatched by Cohen's there and then in February 1966. Presumably the tender was salvaged.

Scrapping in-house was considered to be the most cost-effective option and allowed re-usable items to be removed and stored for

SCRAPPING THE SOUTHERN

the future. Valuable metals such as copper could be melted down and also re-used and of course it did provide employment for a number of BR staff. No doubt this state of affairs would have continued had not the pace of steam locomotive withdrawals accelerated in the 1960s.

On 27 April 1962 the Railway Observer reported that there were no locomotives awaiting scrapping at Ashford for the first time in many years although seven were in the shops for attention. "*Since July 1962 Ashford Works has been employed mainly on the*

overhaul of steam cranes, although Nos 31065 and 30066 have paid brief visits, the latter for renumbering to DS235. Three C Class survive mainly on shunting duties for the wagon works – 31271, 31280, 31592."

The locomotive workshops eventually closed on 16 June 1962, the last locomotive to be repaired at Ashford being N Class No. 31400 on 9 June. The wagon works continued for a further two decades. All loco repair work moved to Eastleigh in June 1962.

Left - No 30901 "Winchester" received the attention of the scrapmen at Eastleigh Works on 7 August 1963. Note the liberal use of ladders to gain access to the running plate. The side of the cab has been cut-through ready to be lifted clear. (Ian Nolan)

Above - On the same date the smokebox numberplate of Q1 No 33005 is freed with an oxyacetylene torch. Alongside is the smokebox formerly belonging to No 30934 "St Lawrence". (Ian Nolan)

SCRAPPING THE SOUTHERN

ASHFORD: 1962 final year of scrapping

Loco	Class	Date
31306	H	6/1/62
31759	L1	6/1/62
32544	C2X	6/1/62
32549	C2X	6/1/62
31739	D1	13/1/62
31749	D1	13/1/62
32438	C2X	13/1/62
32538	C2X	13/1/62
30920	V	20/1/62
30924	V	20/1/62
32500	E4	27/1/62
32525	C2X	3/2/62
32535	C2X	10/2/62
30788	N15	17/2/62
32523	C2X	17/2/62
30326	700	24/2/62
30863	LN	24/2/62
31584	C	3/3/62
32416	E6	3/3/62
30852	LN	10/3/62
31317	C	10/3/62
31717	C	10/3/62
30900	V	17/3/62
30804	N15	24/3/62
30909	V	24/3/62
31530	H	31/3/62
31689	C	7/4/62
32509	E4	7/4/62
32581	E4	14/4/62

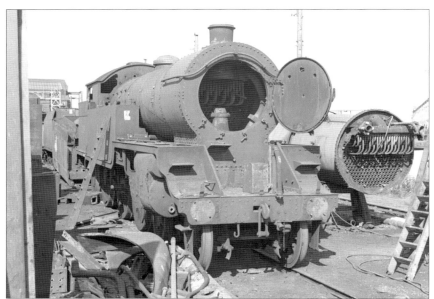

All sizes were dealt with from a small size tank engine to the opposite end of the spectrum, seen here in the form of H16 No 30519 in the main yard at Eastleigh in November 1962. All five of the class had been withdrawn in November and it would appear were despatched rapidly.

Beattie well-tank No 30586, the only one of the trio that did not survive, seen awaiting dismantling. Chalked on the side is a comment that a particular part is required.

(Both Eric Best)

IN-HOUSE SCRAPPING

The mortal remains of A1X No 32661 once named 'Sutton' and viewed from the front framing. Already most of the smokebox, plus the sidetanks and cab have gone. Withdrawn in April 1963 it was then 88 years old and had the dubious distinction of being the final 'Terrier' to be cut up. The view was taken at the rear of Eastleigh Works with the coppersmith's shop in the right background.

W class 2-6-4 No 31923 meets its end at Eastleigh in 1963. This was also the first member of the class to be withdrawn. Working on the ladder is regular dismantler Owen whilst walking at the rear of the engine is Dick Mitchell - ex Brighton works.

(Both Eric Best)

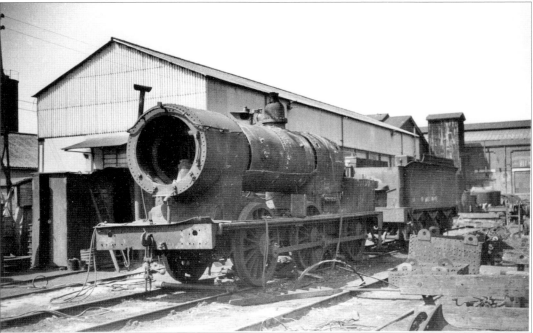

Two last members of their class. Above is Adams 0395 No 30567 in the process of being dismantled at Eastleigh in 1959. (Eric Best)

Left, the final Class 700 in existence, (believed to be No. 30700) late of Exmouth Junction shed where it performed snowplough duties during the ferocious winter of 1962/63 meets its maker at Eastleigh Works in April 1964.
(Ray Rosendale)

IN-HOUSE SCRAPPING

In-house scrapping also took place at Stewarts Lane. It was decided to scrap one of the K Class moguls in situ at the shed in 1963/64.....

Right - Ex London Brighton & South Coast Railway K class mogul, No 32347 has been savaged by the scrapman in the yard of Stewarts Lane shed.

Middle - The bare bones of K class 2-6-0 No 32347 lie piled in front of the shed. Inside the shed are H class No 31305 which was withdrawn at 73A on 30 November 1962 and despatched to Cashmore's at Great Bridge on 31 July 1964 where she was scrapped. Similarly No 31542 was also withdrawn at the Lane on 30 November 1962 and was sent to Ward's, Briton Ferry, on 31 July 1964.

Right- With connecting rods removed, K class 2-6-0 No 32340 awaits the end parked just in the shed.

(This page Barry Lewis)

4. A Scrapman Remembers

Eric Best, in conversation with "The Southern Way", recalls his time scrapping engines at Eastleigh Works between February 1957 and October 1963

TSW *"What is the history of your employment with BR?"* **EB** "I started cutting up in 1957 after National Service, because I could not get on with the chargehand inside ….someone said to me there were a couple of 'Arthurs' out the back that needed cutting up and would I like to a have a go, I could not wait to get out there."

TSW *"Were you aware of the historically important locos you were scrapping e.g. last Brighton Atlantic?"* **EB** "The last Atlantic certainly...that was a lovely engine. They should have saved her...we delayed as long as possible before starting to dismantle it. There were also the frames of the 'Bug', just on bogies...not a lot left really but if they had survived, consider what they can do nowadays…..!"

TSW *"Why did you keep records of locos scrapped?"* **EB** "Ah, that one is easy. We were paid piecework so I could keep a check that I was getting paid properly. Later I kept a record for myself… just for fun really. Somewhere along the line one of those little books has gone missing...shame, as it was the only record."

TSW *"Did you supply details of the engines dismantled to the RCTS?"* **EB** "No, I didn't but I know who did. That was Dave Parfitt who was in the works at the time. He was something to do with the RCTS and would come down to see us to get the details from me which he would then send in."

TSW *"How were the engines moved into the right place for scrapping?"* **EB** "There was a works shunting engine and it would collect engines when necessary and move them into position for us - usually this was after lunch as part of the 'afternoon shunt'."

TSW *"What was the process of notifying you that a loco would be scrapped?"* **EB** "That was easy. If it looked like we were running out of work I would go over to the running shed and see the Foreman there, Jimmy Gibson. I would ask him what had he got and he would send a couple round." (Eric went on to explain that engines that had been condemned would congregate on the 'dump' - two roads at the shed - these were then brought round by the works shunter. He was asked who made the decision to withdraw engines and he admitted he did not know. "Probably some desk wallah - like the time they withdrew all the 'K's - there were years of life left in them, it was criminal.")

TSW *"Did you go to the shed first to remove fittings – if so what were they – before the loco was towed to the back of the works?"* **EB** "Sometimes we did go to the shed to remove fittings...brass and copper was saved and taken back to the works (but not the copper fireboxes). Eastleigh had a contract with certain scrap merchants who would take away the various pieces of the dismantled engines. Most of the time the boilers were lifted off and sent away complete on 'warwells' -

The original No 32424 "Beachy Head" withdrawn and awaiting scrapping. Eric and his colleagues delayed disposing of this engine for as long as possible - in the hope it might be saved - sadly that was not to be. In the right background are the primitive messing facilities available in the form of an old hut. Eric comments the view was taken in summer, hence the outside seat!
(Eric Best)

(bogie well-wagon) to the scrap merchant. Occasionally we might be told to cut up or keep a particular boiler but there was not the room to keep too many. Cutting up a boiler also meant a lot of debris and there was not a lot of room where we worked." (Eric explained the cutting up was always done at the back of the works and in the open air.)

TSW *"Did you salvage any items personally or in response to requests from enthusiasts?"* **EB** "Personally no, there was no one really interested at the time. What I did was to take off the number and nameplates, plus if there was a works plate and the shed-code. These were taken to a small wooden shed outside the front of the works from where I presume they ended up in the stores. No one ever asked us to cut out number panels."

TSW *"What items were kept e.g. boilers, aws etc.?"* **EB** "As I said, the occasional boiler, AWS gear certainly, plus some tenders - some from the Schools ended up as snow-ploughs. I remember one day when we were cutting up a 'Nelson', Harry Frith came rushing down to say he wanted the inside left-hand expansion link for another engine at Basingstoke. There were a few others I remember where the bunker off No (3)2677 was salvaged and later put on No (3)2662. There was also a general swap around of bits from two M7s and a similar situation with the frames from a couple of T9s. Otherwise once it was on the scrapline that was it."

TSW *"How many were employed in the scrapping gang and how many gangs?"* **EB** Just two of us, Dick Mitchell and myself. Later as more and more engines were coming round another pair was involved, but because of the limited room they operated at the back of the wheel-shop."

TSW *"How long did it take to scrap a loco?"* **EB** "We reckoned we could do two a week. The yard gang were also involved as they would load the bits into wagons (not by road) to be taken away….Cohen's was one of the ones where the scrap was sent. In the early 1950s they used to do cutting up on the night shift inside the works at the top of No 4 road. Because there were a lot of oil-burners being cut up at the time the smoke and smell inside the next morning was terrible."

TSW *"What happened to the scrap metal ?"* **EB** "The railway had contracts with a few local firms, most of these were at Southampton, Cohen's, Ward's - the 600 group, the wagons we filled would be taken away to their site."

TSW *"When did you appreciate that scrapping was getting too much for works to handle?"* **EB**"We were kept busy all the time. But then in 1964 one of them

b*****d Bulleid things came round, No 34110. I detested them things….hated dealing with them in the works and hated the look of them. I refused to work on it, even to cut it up, asked for and got a transfer to the running sheds." (No 34043 may well have been cut up beforehand - but not by Eric.)

TSW *"Why did you finish with scrapping activity and what did you move on to?"* **EB** "Well as I said, it was because of them Bulleids, so I moved to the shed as a fitter - but of course over at the running shed I was dealing with them all the time" - at this point Eric's descriptions became a bit more colourful.

TSW *"Were you responsible for the withdrawal of any engines over at the shed?"* **EB** "Only one, and that was a Bulleid, No 35005. It worked a train down and came on shed with a written note referring to chalk marks on the front nearside driving wheel. They had been put there as Nine Elms were suspicious the tyre was moving on the wheel, when I looked at the marks they had moved. That was the end for that one. I had left the railway before the end of steam."

TSW *"When you were scrapping what tools did you have?"* **EB** "My mate Dick Mitchell was an ex-Brighton man and he used the oxy-acetylene torch. I had a hammer and chisel. Later, as there was more and more work, another man was used with a torch. He had the nickname 'Yogi Bear' and came from Ashford."

TSW *"What were the working hours?"* **EB** "Long and cold. Apart from Dick and Yogi who had goggles and what were called 'Zoot' suits of white asbestos, there was no safety gear or weather protection at all. You just got on with it. Some of the engines came round with water and coal in the tender, (indicating they had been serviced on shed before the decision was made for withdrawal.) One engine from Salisbury arrived with a fish in the tank, a stone loach, we kept that fish for ages…. Even in the winter of 1962/63 we were outside, there was a small wooden hut we could go into at times but that was it."

TSW *"Did you cut up any engines from other regions?"* **EB** "Only some Pannier Tanks, and that was just the once."

TSW *"Were any engines more difficult than others to scrap – ease of access etc?"* **EB** "They were all the same, the only tricky bit came when the axles were cut in two, then it was a question of cut through and at the last minute jump back - a bit sharpish. There were no accidents that I remember and certainly no protection from the asbestos that blew around. Thinking about it we were lucky to have been working in the open air."

TSW *"Presumably it was physically tiring and arduous work?"* **EB** "Mainly dirty, the only washing facilities we had was a bucket with cold water. We would heat a bolt in the fire (inside the hut) and drop that into the bucket to warm the water. My wife used to moan something rotten about the state of my overalls. We could get water from the signalman at (Eastleigh) South signal box, but we thought it would be easier to tap into his water pipe so we had a supply near to hand. There was a bit of trouble over that."

TSW *"Was there any supervision of your work, visits by inspectors etc?"* **EB** "Nothing at all, no one bothered us, and as we were on piece-work we just got on with it. Neither was there any training, you just got on with it."

TSW *"What do you think of the prices being charged for memorabilia these days – nameplates etc.?"* **EB** "Too silly for words, I only ever bought one nameplate and that was for £15 - sold it later...wish I had bought more….!"

Below - No 34055 "Fighter Pilot" was one of the first in the withdrawal programme of Bulleid pacifics. Having sustained a cracked middle cylinder, it was among the first quartet to be taken out of service in June 1963. It was not scrapped at Eastleigh until the spring of 1964. (The others were Nos 34035/43/74.) (Ray Rosendale)

ENG'S CUT UP BY ME			
CLASS	N°	DATE	NOTES
T9	30732	5/2/58	Frame
O2	30224	11/2/58	
O2	30233	19/2/58	
G6	30162	28/2/58	
M7	30038	6/3/58	
N15	30738	13/3/58	Eng only
M7	30675	21/3/58	
O395	30568	14/4/58	Eng & Tender
O395	30564	26/4/58	Eng Tender
T9	30284	5/5/58	"A "
M7	30022	12/5/58	
H2	32424	26/5/58	Eng & Tender
M7	30037	6/6/58	
T9	30285	21/6/58	
H15	30334	13/7/58	
M7	30243	27/9/58	
E1	32113	11/10/58	
T9	30727	18/10/58	

A SCRAPMAN REMEMBERS

Opposite top - Extract from one of Eric's notebooks during his time on the scrapyard. Noteworthy is the entry for 26 May 1958 reference No 32424 the last Brighton Atlantic "Beachy Head", at one time a candidate for preservation. Eric comments, "I had heard rumours that this engine might be preserved - b****y well should have been as well. When she came round to us I made sure we left her intact, in the hope that someone might come out and ask if she was still there. We would cut up everything else but leave this one intact. Eventually we did have to start but even then it was half-hearted, nothing was removed that might have rendered her impossible to save. But it all came to nought and she was despatched the same as all the others....". The last of the class No 32424's swansong had been an enthusiasts' special over the route she had made her own - to Newhaven - on 13 April 1958. After this she went to Brighton before making the trip, in steam, to Eastleigh and withdrawal. Even so she was far from worn out, as this last journey to Eastleigh had been with 12 coaches from Lancing destined for the Carriage Works at Eastleigh.

No. 30496 is devoured in a shower of sparks as scrapmen cling precariously to the boiler top of this withdrawn S15 on 21 August 1963, seen at the rear of Eastleigh Works.

No 31619 reduced to its frames at Eastleigh Works whilst another Maunsell Mogul awaits similar treatment behind. This view was taken in March 1966, scrapping being undertaken by "flying scrappers" from Cohen's as in-house scrapping at Eastleigh had generally finished by this time. (Peter Yarlett)

No 30865 "Sir John Hawkins" was the first Nelson to be scrapped and is seen in a partly dismembered state at Eastleigh Works in June 1961. (Peter Yarlett)

N15 No 30800 "Sir Meleaus de Lile" which was withdrawn the previous month is in the process of being scrapped at Eastleigh Works in September 1961. Eastleigh South signal box (on the line to Fareham) is in the background.

The condemned road outside the back of the running shed. Here engines were stored awaiting either works attention or scrapping. The unidentified Bulleid in the background will not steam again, as testified by the removed nameplate and hole in the casing which formerly housed the crest, but the LMR 8F will. The latter was among a small number of the class that arrived at Eastleigh for overhaul and they were stored until they could be accommodated at the works. Once restored to serviceable condition they were returned to the LMR.

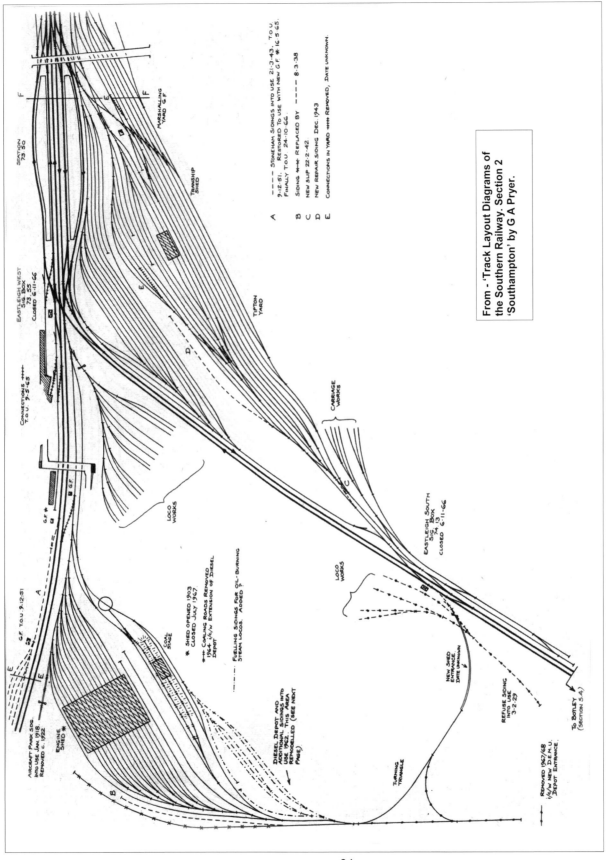

From - 'Track Layout Diagrams of
the Southern Railway. Section 2
'Southampton' by G A Pryer.

Above - Enlarged from the 1945 Ordnance Survey 'one inch' series, the locations of the running sheds and works are shown. Running north to south is the Waterloo to Southampton main line with the Romsey / Salisbury route heading west from a junction north of the actual station. The line to Fareham and Portsmouth bisects the locomotive and carriage works. As can be seen from the enlarged plan of the general area on the opposite page, the north-facing stub end of the triangle was later extended to form a connection back into the Portsmouth line adjacent to Eastleigh South SB.
(Reproduced with permission of the Ordnance Survey)

Right - The layout of the works c1960. Cutting was carried out in the open air at the rear of the works in the area beyond the boiler shop where wheels were also stored in the open air.
(Colin Boocock)

Opposite page - Track layout and triangle / shed access for Eastleigh.

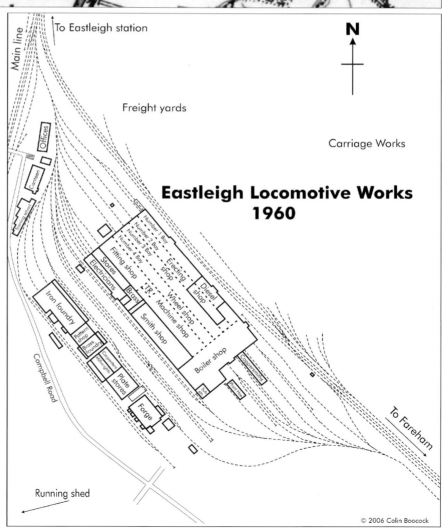

Eastleigh Locomotive Works 1960

© 2006 Colin Boocock

5. Tendering for the Tenders (& the Locomotives Too!)

Transactions were by competitive tender, the highest bid secured the sale, but the scrap merchant usually had to add the cost of movement by rail from the BR site to his yard and this could add as much as £200 to the price although in some cases there was an option indicating "Carriage paid by BR". As transactions increased in number, the locos were no longer sent from BR works but from their home sheds. This broadened the scope considerably as it could reduce the cost of transit and encourage more local yards to bid for locomotives made redundant in their home area. Consequently the number of yards increased and scrapyards became more proficient at handling throughput. It made long distance movements more worthwhile and there were some surprisingly long journeys made by SR locomotives to Rotherham, Norwich and Swansea.

In 1964/5 it was a condition of sale that the copper firebox of a loco sold for scrap to a private yard should be returned to BR. Most went to Derby where, stripped of all foreign metal, they were melted down and re-forged as copper wire for the WCML electrification. Oddly BR did not always reclaim the fireboxes they were entitled to and lines of them, neatly stacked could be seen at scrapyards awaiting collection that never came. Some of the sales correspondence reveals complaints from scrap dealers that often quite significant items were missing from locomotives upon receipt, for example coupling rods, boiler mountings and injectors. Instructions duly went out that each locomotive should be inspected before departure and that under no circumstances should parts be removed for use as spares for other locomotives without prior authority. Items which could be legitimately removed before sale were the nameplate, smokebox door numberplate, the depot allocation plate and the works plates. Of course tenders should have been emptied of coal and boilers emptied of water but again this did not always happen. Where parts were missing they were often located and subsequently sent on e.g. 4 connecting rods, 8 coupling rods and 15 elements from Nos 82015 and 73074 were despatched in a wagon to Cashmore's of Newport in February 1965.

Typical prices for locomotives were approx. £1500 for a small tank engine and approx. £2,000-2,500 for a mainline engine. The examples opposite, where carriage was paid by BR, show that in 1966 a Merchant Navy could be had for £2,015 whilst surprisingly a Standard Class 3 tank was only £10 less and an Ivatt tank came in at £1,300. Where carriage was at the expense of the contractor, typical sums charged were £1,630 for a Standard Class 5 from Nine Elms to Newport, £1,756 for an S15 from Feltham to Newport and £1,430 for a Q1 from Eastleigh to Morriston.

The sale by BR was on the understanding that "*locos and tenders will be broken up*". This was subsequently

Left - 'Reflections on Southern Steam'. Two former Bulleid types, once proudly displaying the names 'Ilfracombe' and 'Elder Dempster Lines' await their fate at Cashmore's yard, Newport on 1 November 1968. No 34017 had not quite survived until the end of steam, being withdrawn in October 1966, No 35030 however had the distinction of hauling the last steam hauled train into Waterloo on Sunday 9 July 1967, after which it languished first at Nine Elms, then at Salisbury before being towed to South Wales to await its fate here. Neither would survive much longer.

Opposite top right - Ironically one of the sales referred to, No 35029, would return to national ownership after purchase from Woodhams by the NRM for display in sectional form at York.

Document 1 (top left)

BRITISH RAILWAYS   BR 8688

Order No. 230/522T/55.

.... Motive Power .... Dept.

.... Nine Elms .... Station

Date ...... 19.2.1965. ......

I have to-day despatched the undermentioned material from
Nine Elms M.P. Depot ...... to Messrs. John Cashmore, Ltd.,
Newport, Monmouthshire.

in accordance with your instructions bearing the above order number.

To the SUPPLIES AND CONTRACTS MANAGER,
SALES SECTION, 29 ADDINGTON ST.,
YORK ROAD, LONDON, S.E.1.

Material	Actual or computed quantity or weight (stating which)	Truck No.	For Stores Accounts use only			
			Rate Per Ton	£	s.	d.
73074 and 82015 despatched via Eastleigh.						
4 Connecting Rods. } 8 Coupling Rods. } 15 Elements. }	*about* Ex/Condemned Locos No's 82015 & 73074.					
Wagon No. B.278420.						

Document 2 (top right)

Eversholt House
Eversholt Street
London NW1
Euston 3414.

British Railways Board

Chief Supplies and Contracts Officer

Woodham Brothers,
54a, Thompson Street,
Barry,
Glam.

y/r
o/r

17/230/522T/266

CME S

Date

Dear Sir/s,   3rd. November 1966

Sales Reference 230/

I am pleased to advise you that your offer to purchase
the following has been accepted subject to the terms and
conditions shown on my tender form.   XXXXXX 17/230/522T/266

Loco.No.	Location.	Destination.	Rate of Acceptance.	Price each Carriage Paid by British Railways to the nearest available Station or Sidings to your Works.
35010	Nine Elms	Barry	Immediate	£2,015. 0. 0d.
35029	"	"	"	£2,015. 0. 0d.
35027	"	"	"	£2,015. 0. 0d.
82006	"	"	"	£2,005. 0. 0d.

This acceptance is issued on the understanding that locos and tenders will be broken up.

Chief Mechanical & Electrical Engineer, British Railways, Southern Region,
Records Office, ... lesley Grove, Croydon, Surrey.

Terms :- Payment on Delivery.

Please send full consigning instructions to the :-

Yours faithfully,

for R.B. HOFF.

Document 3 (bottom left)

British Railways   BR 4/2

y/r
date

to   Divisional Manager,
      South Western Division.

      Copy to: ...... Flutter, Esq.

o/r date   J.9/11/0-(4)
            15th November, 1966.

from   General Manager,
            Waterloo.

ext   2574

CONDEMNED LOCOMOTIVES

Confirming telephone conversation of the 5th November, 1966.
The undermentioned locomotives have now been accepted for
sale and I shall be pleased if you will arrange for these to be
despatched as quickly as possible.

Number	Depot	Destination	Firm
41301	Weymouth	Private Sidings Beaufort Works Morriston	G. Cohen Sons & Co. Ltd.
75070	Eastleigh	Town Dock Newport. Mon.	J. Cashmore Ltd.
35010	Nine Elms	Barry, Glam.	Woodham Brothers.
35027	"	"	"
35029	"	"	"
82006	"	"	"

Will you please arrange for the removal of all coal, water
and detonators from the locomotives prior to being sent to their
destination.

Detailed consigning instructions and despatch advice
requirements are being issued direct to the depots from the Materials
& Progressing Section.

Document 4 (bottom right)

GEORGE COHEN SONS & COMPANY LIMITED

Telephone: Shepherds Bush 2070
Telegrams: Coborn London
Telex: 21288/9

★ 600 WOOD LANE
LONDON W.12

Your Ref: 17/230/522T/266.
Our Ref: TTS/PB.

9th November 1966.

Chief Mechanical & Electrical Engineer,
British Railways, (Southern Region,
Records Office,
Southern House,
Wellesley Grove,
CROYDON, SURREY.

Dear Sir,

Sales Ref. 17/230/522T/266

You will no doubt have been informed that we have been successful in
purchasing the undermentioned locomotive:-

Loco No.	Location	Destination
41301	Weymouth	Morriston.

The above Locomotive should be despatched immediately to:-

GEORGE COHEN SONS & COMPANY LIMITED.,
  Private Sidings,
  Beaufort Works,
  MORRISTON,
  SWANSEA, GLAM.

Yours faithfully,
For: GEORGE COHEN SONS & COMPANY LIMITED.

T. P. Steeley.

End of the line for No 41301 in store at Weymouth and subsequently reduced to a despatch docket of 63 tons of scrap! (JG)

relaxed such that re-sale of locomotives was only permitted by a scrapyard subject to a levy placed upon the sale. Woodham's for example set the price for each locomotive at its exact scrap value (each type had an exact metal content breakdown from BR, so this was simply taken and multiplied by that day's scrap rate for each metal component), plus the BR levy; with the sale price completed by the addition of VAT, initially set at 10% but raised to 15% in 1979. For most of the time that locomotives were being 'rescued' from Barry, it became accepted commercial practice by the company for preservation groups to pay a deposit for a particular locomotive, which was then given "protected/reserved" status until the group could pay for the locomotive in full and arrange transport. In practice this meant that parts continued to be stolen, the large site being very open and insecure.

BR. 8658

MATERIALS SOLD BY
BRITISH RAILWAYS BOARD
Southern Region

Reference SALES 17/230/5221/226

Item No.

ADVICE OF DESPATCH

Date of Sale 3-11-66

Departmental Accountant (Title)

Date 5-1-67

Serial No.

COPY No. 4

TO BE RETAINED BY ISSUING OFFICE

PURCHASER:— George Cohen Sons & Co LTD.
600, Wood Lane,
London, W.12.

DESPATCHED FROM Motive Power _____ Department
Weymouth _____ Works/Depot

TO (Name of Consignee) George Cohen Sons & Co Ltd,
Destination station or siding Private Sidings, Beaufort Works, Morriston, Glam

* Carriage charges payable by purchaser. Consignment note passed to Goods Agent.
* Carriage paid by B.R. Free Invoice/Waybill passed to Goods Agent.
* Delete whichever is inapplicable.

CATALOGUE No.
MATERIAL Locomotive No 41301

Date of Despatch	TRUCK		QUANTITY DESPATCHED														
	Prefix Letter	No.	No. of Articles	Gross				Tare				Net			
				T	C	Q	lb.	T	C	Q	lb.	T	C	Q	lb.
5-1-67	Locomotive														
	No 41301											63	—	—	—
TOTALS (If more than one entry):—																

Signature
Shed Master

6. Down in the Dumps

Withdrawn locomotives were traditionally sent to the nearest works for scrapping but when the volume of withdrawals exceeded the capacity of Works to deal with them, then any available siding space was used for temporarily housing this withdrawn stock. A number of locations on the SR were used, often adjacent to engine sheds, but sometimes where siding space was available, such as in Hove Goods Yard. Locomotives from Brighton shed were brought here for varying periods before despatch to Eastleigh Works for scrapping.

Fratton also played host to withdrawn locomotives and for a time also housed those examples laid aside for preservation. M7 No 30245, N15 No 30777, LN No 30850, T9 No 120 and O298 No 30587 were all to be found here at one time before dispersal to other storage locations. Additionally some locomotives that were considered worthy candidates for preservation, but which for some reason did not make it, were also stored here, examples being Z Class No 30952 and L1 Class No 31757.

Following the end of steam on the SR in July 1967, Salisbury and Weymouth depots were chosen to house withdrawn locomotives. The train traveller going west today from Salisbury to Exeter or Bristol may perhaps casually glance to the south of the tracks about half a mile after leaving the station and wonder what used to occupy an area of waste ground now fenced off and covered with scrub. To the initiated, of course, this was once the site of what was formerly known as 72B, latterly 70E, namely Salisbury Motive Power Depot. This now demolished 10-road structure was once home to over 80 engines encompassing a wide variety of SR locomotives from the humble M7 tanks to the mighty Bulleid pacifics. It was surrounded by a high wall on two sides pierced only by a set of steps leading to the one entrance which the unwary enthusiast had to negotiate by crouching down to pass under the window of the shed office. It was a notoriously difficult shed to "bunk" without a permit and I was summarily ejected after only having completed a couple of rows of engines on the few occasions that I managed to get inside in steam days.

After 9 July 1967 it was to be very different

History of Hove Dump (December 1962 – June 1963)			
Class	No.	Movements	Scrapped
E6	32417	Arrived December. Removed to Brighton April.	October 1963
E6	32418	Arrived December. Towed to Brighton 12 March. Towed to Eastleigh 18 May.	July 1963
Schools	30901 Winchester	Arrived December	August 1963
Schools	30911 Dover	Arrived December. Towed to Brighton 1 June .	September 1963
Schools	30915 Brighton	Arrived December	November 1963
Schools	30916 Whitgift	Arrived February	September 1963
Schools	30923 Bradfield	Arrived December. Left in June	August 1963
K	32338	Arrived December	September 1963
K	32341	Arrived December. Removed to Brighton April	August 1963
U1	31891	Arrived February. Departed March	July 1963
U1	31895	Arrived February. Removed to Brighton April	August 1963
E4	32474	Arrived December. Restored to traffic 12 January 1963	June 1963
E4	32479	Arrived December. Restored to traffic 12 January 1963.	July 1963
E4	32468	Arrived March	August 1963
N1	31876	Arrived 4 June. Departed for Brighton 27 July.	October 1963

SCRAPPING THE SOUTHERN

however, for live steam finished on the Southern on that date followed by the introduction of electric services on the Waterloo - Bournemouth line. Along with Weymouth, the shed and associated sidings at Salisbury were then used to store the redundant steam locomotive fleet that the SR wished to be shot of as soon as possible. They were farmed out to these extremities of the network ostensibly to be as close as possible to South Wales, where the majority of yards that were to take their allocation of BR scrap was located. Conveniently they were out of sight (and so out of mind) to most of the region's passengers and therefore did not conflict with the modern image that the Southern wished to cultivate in the post-steam era.

Top - Part of the line up in Hove Goods yard, Nos 32338, 30923 and 30911 sit out the severe winter of 1962/3. (Ian Nolan)

Bottom - Here No 30911 has arrived back at Brighton shed on 1 June 1963 after having been extracted from the dump in Hove Goods Yard prior to making its final journey to Eastleigh Works. Maunsell N Class mogul No 31829 is behind the Schools. (Charlie Verrall)

Final Days at Nine Elms. Some of the last locomotives left at the depot await departure on 26 August 1967. For the record they were Nos 35007, 34034 and 34008 marshalled in the yard ready to leave. The photographer recorded that also on shed that day were Nos 34013, 35023, 35008, 35030, 34001 and D3047. The grass grown tracks tell their own story. (Jonathan Martin)

Redundant Southern steam power at Salisbury, stored and awaiting disposal. Around 50 locomotives were concentrated here. Nearest the camera are Nos 34056, 30064 and 30072.

Left - The rear of Redhill shed in February 1963 with Nos 30930 'Radley' and U1 31900, among others, under a blanket of snow.
(Charlie Verrall)

Bottom - No 31876 chalk marked "For Redhill Scrap Heap" is seen there on 1 June 1963.
(Charlie Verrall)

Weymouth dump seen in the autumn of 1967. Whitewashed buffers and hinges were the trademark embellishments of several locomotives towards the end. (JG)

With crest and nameplate crudely removed through the expedient of cutting through the air-smoothed casing, No 34084 "253 Squadron'" waits for its inevitable demise at Weymouth on 14 November 1965, having been withdrawn from Eastleigh shed the previous month. The fact it was here indicates a possible shortage of storage space at Eastleigh. (JG)

In store at Salisbury are Standard tanks Nos 80133 and 80152 together with a pair of USA tanks. (JG)

A contrast in front ends seen on Weymouth dump. (JG)

DOWN IN THE DUMPS

A personal recollection by Jeffery Grayer:

Salisbury's own allocation of locomotives, which had reduced dramatically following the WR dieselisation of the Exeter route in 1964, was down to just 23 by 1966 and was further depleted to a dozen by January 1967, reduced finally to just three Bulleid pacifics by July. Concurrent with its own operational allocation diminishing, the depot began to receive engines for storage which had been withdrawn elsewhere, until such time as a completed sale resulted in the call to the scrapyard. Typical of such arrivals were Nos 73037, 34057 "Biggin Hill" and 80085 which were towed from Nine Elms behind D6576 on 20 April 1967.

The pace of arrivals picked up during the first week of July 1967 when locomotives from the other remaining SR steam sheds, namely Guildford (9 allocated in July), Eastleigh (21), Nine Elms (25) and Bournemouth (15) began to arrive. Many of these locos went under their own steam either singly or in pairs, all part of the run down of their home sheds. Those that were too weak to manage it by themselves had perforce to be towed. The majority of stock from Bournemouth shed tended to migrate westwards to Weymouth, however this did depend to some extent upon where the locomotives found themselves on their last day of service. For example 10 of Bournemouth's fleet were to be stored at Salisbury, whilst five from Guildford and four from Eastleigh ended up on Weymouth's scraplines.

Eastleigh had no stragglers on hand after 9 July, indeed travelling past on the first day of the full electric service, Monday 10 July, the shed could already be seen as empty, the men told to remove all they needed as demolition started immediately. (The site occupied by the former steam shed at Eastleigh was converted into the same number of sidings as had existed before, although now for rolling stock. It continues to perform the same function nearly fifty years later.)

There was no such urgency at Nine Elms, which still had over 30 engines in the middle of July and held on to some of its former stock for several weeks longer. Six locomotives made the trip to Salisbury during the last week of July and first week of August but there still remained 22 now rusting steam engines on shed in the capital on 9 August. After this, a regular working left Nine Elms at 15.38 on Sundays for the next few weeks with a Crompton diesel hauling two or three dead locomotives at a time. On 27 August D6555 was in charge of Nos 34008 "Padstow", 34034 "Honiton" and 35007 "Aberdeen Commonwealth". A week later D6517 towed Nos 34001 "Exeter", 34013

"Okehampton" and 35030 "Elder Dempster Lines". On 10 September the final steam stock was hauled away to Salisbury when D6549 took Nos 35023 "Holland - Afrika Line" and 34088 "213 Squadron". Although these workings deliberately took place on a Sunday when other traffic was light, they did not always go to plan, for stock that had not moved for a while and which was not being maintained was notoriously prone to hot boxes. Such a case stopped No 34034 en route to Salisbury as early as Surbiton where it had to be detached. Two weeks later it had been towed as far as Basingstoke where it remained for several weeks in splendid isolation, the last true resident of Basingstoke shed, No 80151, having made the trip to Salisbury at the end of July.

To begin with, none of the Merchant Navy Class could be seen on Salisbury's dump as the last eight working examples were allocated to Nine Elms at the end. However, with the exception of the preserved No 35028 "Clan Line" and, strangely, No 35012 "United States Line" (withdrawn in April 1967), which travelled to Weymouth, the rest did make their way down to the weed-choked sidings at Salisbury.

For a while arrivals exceeded departures such that the amount of stock continued to increase at Salisbury until the maximum was probably reached in early August, when the count was in the mid 50s. Thereafter numbers began to decline as deals were struck and locomotives were taken in stages, again in small numbers, all to South Wales. The route taken was usually via Warminster, Westbury, Bristol, Gloucester and Severn Tunnel Junction, invariably ending at Newport where the premises of Messrs Cashmore and Buttigieg were located. In spite of precautions hot boxes were again to hold up these mournful convoys on occasion with, for example No 34002 "Salisbury" being stuck at Gloucester's Horton Road shed for a while following development of a hot box at Coaley Junction. (Note: as far as is known none travelled through the Severn Tunnel.) Whilst there, a gang of enthusiasts descended upon the locomotive giving it a thorough polishing, white painted buffers and lamp brackets and artistically reinstating the name, crest and smokebox number thereby ensuring it looked its best for the scrapmen.

The opportunity was taken to exhibit a couple of Bulleids travelling this well worn path at Bristol's Bath Road Diesel Depot Open Day on 21 October 1967. I attended this event and, apart from being able to buy a selection of S & D tickets and the Book of Distances from Radstock North station used to calculate freight rates, I particularly remember seeing No 34013 "Okehampton" and No 34100 "Appledore" lined up for inspection, both in reasonable external condition.

The steady procession of locomotives made their way to South Wales from both Weymouth and Salisbury as the summer waned. Typical of such movements was the aforementioned No 34002 which was noted at the end of some freight wagons in a siding outside Bath Spa on 26 August, whilst three days later Nos 34017 "Ilfracombe", 34019 "Bideford" and 73119 were seen at Severn Tunnel Junction. No 34040 "Crewkerne" was noted passing Rangeworthy on 1 October in company with No 34001 "Exeter", both being hauled by the rather aptly named Warship diesel D860 "Victorious". Three weeks later they had still only reached Severn Tunnel Junction. Moving forward Nos 75076, 76007, 76026 and 76031 were seen at Gloucester on 15 October as were Nos 80016 and 80085 on 29 October.

Some of the stock from the other SR collection point, Weymouth, was transferred to Salisbury rather than being taken direct to South Wales via Castle Cary and the Western Region. Typical of such movement was that of No 76008 which was noted at Branksome being towed by D6524 on 7 October en route to Salisbury. December saw the total remaining at Salisbury reduce to 30 with a further fall to 28 by early February 1968. Engineering work in the Gloucester area held up the transfer of withdrawn stock to South Wales in late February with Nos 34036 "Westward Ho",34052 "Lord Dowding",73020 and 76029 stuck in the diesel depot there on 25 March. On 13 March the 09.00 Gloucester - Newport (Alexandra Dock Junction) goods conveyed Nos 30071, 34087 "45 Squadron", 73043 and 73118. The following Sunday saw No 30071 in company with classmates Nos 30067 and 30069, 34018 "Axminster" and ER J94 68012 at Severn Tunnel Junction. The same day Nos 34024 "Tamar Valley", 34060 "25 Squadron" and 34089 "602 Squadron" were at Gloucester.

I made a couple of pilgrimages to Salisbury to photograph the sad lines of withdrawn stock at the shed and in a siding at the east end of the station No 34006 "Bude" was in a sorry state, a far cry from its prestigious days during the 1948 Locomotive Exchanges. March 30 1968 was to see the last movement of stock from Salisbury when the final trio consisting of Nos 34102 "Lapford", appropriately enough the last unmodified Bulleid to see service, 35023 and 34034, the hot box casualty from Basingstoke, were all towed away by Hymek D7045. So, some nine months after the last fires had died on the SR, the final sad remnants of a once great steam fleet were quietly disposed of.

Not all of Salisbury's residents were to end up as scrap however, for amongst their numbers were five USA tanks, a popular engine with fledgling preservation societies in view of their size, power and relatively low purchase price. Nos 30064 and 30072 were both plucked from the scrapline and now grace the Bluebell and the KWVR respectively. No 30064 was sold in December 1967 first moving to Droxford, on the former Meon Valley line stub. It then passed to Liss but following the collapse of the preservation scheme there went ultimately to Sheffield Park, arriving on 24 October 1971. No 30072 was moved by road to Haworth on 14 January 1968. None of the Bulleids survived for the simple reason that none ended up at Barry. Of the other stock only two, Ivatt tank No 41312 (Mid-Hants) and Standard tank No 80151 (Bluebell), were lucky enough to avoid the clutches of the scrapman. In addition, two locomotives stored at Nine Elms were also destined for better things, namely Nos 34023 "Blackmore Vale" and 35028 "Clan Line". None of the residents of Weymouth was saved.

Today all is quiet on the site of 70E where rosebay willow herb grows rank and the weeds flourish, the long lines of withdrawn locomotives now but a distant memory. The wall still bounds the site on two sides and the bricked up staff entrance is still apparent where, more than 35 years ago, I and countless other enthusiasts no doubt tried to gain entrance to one of the Southern Region's last steam bastions.

Weymouth, coded 70G, fulfilled a similar if secondary role in collecting together unwanted SR steam power. Never stabling as much stock as Salisbury and having lost its own allocation of steam in April 1967 when its remaining Merchant Navy Pacifics were transferred to Nine Elms and its Standards to Guildford, it reached a maximum holding of 25 or so and thus was to be emptied sooner than was the case with 70E. I visited the shed both prior to and after that fateful July day to record the scene. By 20 September numbers were down to 20. On 9 December two special trains were run hauling firstly Nos 34004 "Yeovil", 35003 "Royal Mail" and 73018 and subsequently Nos 34036, 34052, 73020, 76069 from Weymouth, once more destined for Newport and similarly via Gloucester. By the end of January 1968 Weymouth had been completely cleared, the last movement sending Nos 34093 "Saunton", 34095 "Brentor", 73092 and 76009 to Cashmore's yard at Newport.

Today the site of 70G is a housing estate and I'm sure many of the current residents have no idea what previously occupied the area. South West Trains electric units and DMUs to Bristol are the staple motive

DOWN IN THE DUMPS

power that now pass the site which was once one of the pair of collection points for redundant SR steam that, with the passage of time, have assumed their rightful place of importance in the annals of Southern Steam.

TABLE 1

LOCATION OF WITHDRAWN STOCK

SALISBURY MPD   29 JULY 1967

USA Tank	5
WC/BB	16
IVATT Tank	1
STANDARD 73XXX	9
STANDARD 75XXX	2
STANDARD 76XXX	9
STANDARD 80XXX	10
STANDARD 82XXX	2
TOTAL	54

In a siding at the east end of the station were 3 WC/BB and 1 Standard 76XXX.

NINE ELMS MPD   22 JULY 1967

WC/BB	12
MN	7
IVATT Tank	3
STANDARD 73XXX	3
STANDARD 75XXX	1
STANDARD 76XXX	1
STANDARD 80XXX	4
TOTAL	31

WEYMOUTH MPD   29 JULY 1967

WC/BB	5
MN	3
IVATT Tank	4
STANDARD 73XXX	5
STANDARD 75XXX	2
STANDARD 76XXX	3
STANDARD 77XXX	1
STANDARD 80XXX	2
TOTAL	25

Green liveried USA tank No. 30064 and classmate 30072 seen on Salisbury scraplines. Both were to enjoy lives in preservation. (JG)

7. "SCHOOLS OUT COMPLETELY" – THE FATE OF A CLASS

Schools out for summer
Schools out for ever
Schools been blown to pieces
Schools out ....completely!
Alice Cooper 1972

In this section we examine the fate of one class of locomotive, Maunsell's famous "Schools". Thirty-four of the forty members were to be scrapped in house, with three further examples being handled by an outside scrap contractor, leaving just three examples to be preserved.

We begin our story in the autumn of 1960 when no fewer than nine "Schools" were receiving attention of one sort or another in Ashford Works. The last to receive a general overhaul here was No 30926 "Repton" in October. The poor state of the boiler of No 30909 gave rise to speculation that this was likely to be the first "Schools" casualty. Surprisingly, in November, a heavy repair was sanctioned and "St Paul's" soldiered on until February 1962. At this stage there did not seem to be any real prospect that wholesale withdrawal of the class was being seriously contemplated, even though it was beginning to prove difficult to find appropriate steam duties in sufficient numbers to keep all members of the class occupied. However, it was known that official policy was to reduce steam stock and to utilise the relatively new Standard Class 5s wherever possible. To add to the problems, the 21 ton axle loading of the "Schools" meant that they were far more restricted than, for example, the more numerous and versatile Bulleid Light Pacifics. As was to be the case with the "Lord Nelsons", their eventual withdrawal from traffic was to prove to be simply a case of redundancy rather than life-expired machinery. Although some members of the class were thirty years old, their mileage was quite modest at between 1m and 1.2m miles, which averaged out at approximately 40,000 miles per year. This compared favourably with other younger classes, for example Merchant Navy's, some of which had already run over 1 million miles by 1961.

That year opened with five examples based at Nine Elms (70A), three at Guildford (70C) and three at Basingstoke (70D). The South Eastern Division still retained four at Stewarts Lane (73A) eight at Bricklayers Arms (73B) and eight at Ashford (73F) with the Central Division having nine allocated to Brighton (75A). The first three months of the year saw three examples transferred from the South Eastern Division

to Feltham shed where their stay was short, for one month later they were transferred to Nine Elms. Redhill gained one of the 4-4-0s in August followed by two more in early 1962, to supplement those already at Guildford, on Reading line services.

Duties on which the "Schools" found themselves were varied but, as mentioned above, their prestige turns were now largely behind them. In May 1961 Tonbridge had Nos 30928/34/35/36 on loan for use on Brighton line trains via Uckfield, a choice which was popular with crews on these heavily loaded trains. The Kent Coast electrification had a knock-on effect throughout the SR's locomotive fleet, the more modern examples being transferred westwards with the older classes being withdrawn. Consequently several "Schools" were used to operate Waterloo-Basingstoke-Salisbury semi-fasts, Nine Elms and Basingstoke's allocation eventually accounting for over half the class in 1961/62. Their range also encompassed trips to Weymouth, where 30921 was noted on the 11:22 service from Waterloo on 28 July 1962 and semi-fast services from Salisbury to Yeovil Junction where 30921 was seen on 25 August 1962. Exeter was still occasionally reached until the end of the summer service as witness the arrival of 30925 with the 10:15 from Waterloo on 27 August and 30934 heading the first portion of the up ACE on 30 August, although it reportedly reached London 50 minutes down. "Schools" moved to duties on the Bournemouth line and in particular were used on Boat Trains from Waterloo to Weymouth, Southampton Docks and to Lymington Pier, taking the latter trains as far as Brockenhurst, Nos 30935/36/37 were noted in use on Lymington trains on just one Saturday in July 1962.

Their time in Kent was not quite done however, and they were to make a surprise return to their old haunts. In response to problems being experienced with the availability of several N1 and Standard tank locomotives, Tonbridge shed borrowed Nos 30917/23/29 in March/April 1962 to work diagrams such as the circular 06:49 from Tonbridge to Hastings followed by the 08:34 Hastings – Ashford and 09:30 Ashford – Tonbridge. The class had been steadily migrating from South Eastern sheds throughout 1961 and by the end of the year they had all gone, primarily to Brighton, Redhill, Nine Elms and Basingstoke, the last to leave, in December 1961, being Nos 30929 and 30930 from Bricklayer's Arms.

On the Central section they operated services from

Happier times. No 30901 "Winchester" at Millbrook on a Bournemouth to Brighton working, 30 August 1958. (Peter Cleare)

Victoria to Brighton via Tunbridge Wells West and less successfully the 07:17 Brighton – London Bridge and 16:40 return on which they developed a habit of stalling on Falmer Bank coming out of Lewes and were consequently replaced by Bulleids in early 1962. Perhaps the route with which they became particularly identified at this time was that from Redhill to Reading, three examples having been allocated to Guildford (30903/06/09) and three to Redhill (30911/24/30) in connection with these trains. I can recall seeing them being serviced on Reading Southern shed at this time. The other memorable train with which they were associated was the 17:25 heavily laden commuter service from London Bridge to Reading and Tonbridge which divided at Redhill. Prestigious duties still occasionally came their way, such as handling the Royal Train from London to Tattenham Corner for the Derby, which a spotless "Repton" powered in 1961 and for the last time on 6 June 1962. The following year, the final time the train was to be steam hauled, a Bulleid Pacific took over.

Of course there were enthusiast railtours to be undertaken, particularly when it became obvious that their days were numbered. In 1962 "Schools" were out on railtour duty on at least five occasions:-

7 January No 30901 Eastleigh-Salisbury-Westbury-Swindon Works-Reading-Eastleigh

25 February LCGB "Kentish Venturer" 30926 handling the leg from Appledore-Ashford-Tonbridge-Orpington-Charing Cross

13 May RCTS "East Midlander" a rare trip to foreign metals when 30926 coupled to ex LMS 2P No 40646 ran from Nottingham – Darlington with a high speed return via York achieving a maximum of 83.5 mph for 3.5 miles on the famous "racing ground".

7 October RCTS "Sussex Special" No 30925 London Bridge – Brighton giving enthusiasts a last chance to see a "Schools" at the head of an express with a timing of 60 minutes for the run (it actually took 64 minutes with seven coaches, although seven minutes were put down to delays).

11 November Home Counties Railway Society No 30926 with T9 No 120 Waterloo – Eastleigh – Havant – Guildford – Waterloo.

The first withdrawals came early in 1961 when Nos 30919 and 30932 were officially condemned in

No 30923 "Bradfield" outside the back of Eastleigh Works awaiting its end. (Ian Nolan)

February. A short period of storage at Ashford Works followed with both locomotives being scrapped there very promptly in March and August respectively. The next to go, in June, was No 30939 with three more, 30904 / 14 / 38 condemned the following month. By the year's end a further nine, Nos 30905 / 7 / 8 / 10 / 18 / 20 / 22 / 31 / 33, had gone leaving just 25 to see in the new year. A further five, Nos 30900 / 09 / 13 / 24 / 27, went in January and February and then there was something of a lull until the winter. Indeed work was still occasionally being done on some members of the class, such as the fitting of AWS equipment to No 30906 at Ashford Works in May. But this stay of execution was not to last.

General retrenchment in 1962 together with a downward drift of freight traffic enabled about 50 type-3 diesel locomotives to be transferred from the South Eastern to the Central and South Western divisions. This influx of new motive power sounded the death knell not only for the "Schools" but also for the "Lord Nelsons" and was to see off the last remaining "King

Arthurs". Even the first of the Bulleids would go the following summer so it seemed that no class was immune. Mention of the Nelsons reminds me that No 30912 received an 8-wheel tender from condemned Nelson 30865 "Sir John Hawkins" in June ostensibly to give additional braking power when working freight trains, not a type of work to which they were particularly suited in any event. It was the intention that others would be similarly treated as the Nelsons were progressively withdrawn. As things turned out, however, only No 30921, which received the tender from No 30854 "Howard of Effingham" in November, was to benefit from this policy. It was not deemed worthwhile to treat any more examples in view of the imminent demise of the "Schools" themselves plus the fact that there continued to be more suitable freight locomotives readily available. One of the "Schools" tenders thereby released was noted on May 20 at Basingstoke attached to S15 No 30833 of Feltham shed, another later recipient being No 30837.

As the number of "Schools" was reduced and work for

them dried up so they became relegated to lesser duties such as the Waterloo – Woking parcels on which Nos 30926 / 36 were noted in October and 30902 / 21 in November 1962. However, heavy passenger work was still occasionally available to them even at this eleventh hour such as No 30934's handling of a Salisbury relief to the 18:00 Waterloo – Exeter on 16 November and No 30925's substitution for a Bulleid on the 17:09 Waterloo – Basingstoke on 2 November. Many examples were to be seen operating minus nameplates at this time, a sure sign of impending withdrawal. But no one could have foreseen quite how swift the end would be.

Withdrawal of Nos 30912 / 17 / 28 in November gave no hint of what was to come the following month when at a stroke the last remaining 17 members of the class were axed. By no means all of this last group were in operational condition for several had been languishing unserviceable at the back of various sheds for some time. This cull was generally seen as an accounting move implemented to reduce steam stocks prior to the replacement of the British Transport Commission by the British Railways Board at the beginning of 1963. A similar fate befell the ex LBSCR K Class moguls, a class which had survived virtually intact, with only two withdrawals the previous month, until December when the remainder of this 17 strong class were summarily withdrawn. In fact 63 locomotives were withdrawn by the Southern Region that month, rendering Classes V, K, Z, E6, H16, 700 and 0298 extinct. One of the last sightings of a Schools on the Central Division had been of No 30911 on the 07:27 Reading to London Bridge on 28 December then taking the 16:40 London Bridge – Brighton via Oxted service. The following day the same engine was unceremoniously despatched from Brighton shed to the dumping ground at Hove Goods Yard in company with Nos 30901, 30915 and 30923.

Nature was to conspire against the railways in January 1963 when snow brought chaos to many lines from Devon to Kent. Despite a directive that those locomotives withdrawn the previous month were under no circumstances to be used in service again, this did in fact happen. In response to the weather emergency Class 700 Nos 30689/97 were resuscitated to assist with snowplough duties on the Exeter --Plymouth line and indeed became stranded in drifts near Okehampton for four days! Rumour has it that some "Schools" were also pressed into service during this period although details have not come to light. It would be intriguing to know whether this was in fact the case. The erstwhile duties of the "Schools" on the Reading – Redhill line were assumed by Standard Class 5s from Stewarts Lane in the new year and West Country

pacifics Nos 34012 "Launceston" and 34019 "Bideford" were noted on the former "Schools" turn, the17:25 London Bridge – Redhill/Reading, in January 1963.

It was with a sense of shock that enthusiasts learnt of the scale of the December slaughter, tinged with regret that they would no longer be able to see these fine machines in action. My own memories of them include No 30901 "Winchester" in steam on Brighton shed where I also recall No 30900 "Eton" languishing unserviceable for several months before being taken away to Ashford for scrapping. I saw them occasionally on through trains from Brighton to Bournemouth and on Eastleigh shed where I photographed 30934 "St Lawrence", complete with nameplates, in the summer of 1962 being held awaiting the final call. 30934 was in fact to be the last example steamed in BR service when, as late as 18 May 1963, it hauled a dead 700 Class from Basingstoke shed to Eastleigh.

The "Schools" came to be stored at a variety of locations after withdrawal, most notably in Hove Goods Yard, Ashford Works, Eastleigh Works, Stewarts Lane and Nine Elms. Between them Ashford and Eastleigh Works were responsible for scrapping no less than 34 of the class. Two of the "Schools" scrapped at Ashford, Nos 30922 / 31, together with seven other Southern locos, were cut into large pieces and travelled to Swinton near Rotherham in November 1961 for final disposal. Only three, Nos 30902 / 21 / 35, were sold to outside contractors, in this case George Cohen & Co. of Kettering, who promptly despatched them in April/May 1964. (Further details are contained in Section 11.)

This left the three survivors who have had varied careers in preservation. Although initially it was understood that the doyen of the class No 30900 "Eton" was earmarked for preservation by BR, in the event it was decided that No 30925 "Cheltenham" would represent the class in the National Collection. This decision reflected not only the state of No 30900, stored for many months in poor condition at Brighton but also the fact that it was not in original condition having been modified by the fitting of a multiple jet blastpipe. After an appearance at Rocket 150 No 30925 spent some time stuffed and mounted at the NRM but has now been returned to steam on long term loan to the Mid-Hants Railway. No 30926 "Repton", after a period of storage at Fratton depot and restoration at Eastleigh Works, went abroad to the Steamtown Foundation at Swallow Falls, Virginia, USA but was subsequently repatriated and is now on the NYMR. No 30928 "Stowe" was purchased by Lord Montagu for his museum at Beaulieu and moved there in March 1964 in company with three Pullman cars

No 30916 "Whitgift" is seen at the rear of Eastleigh shed in September 1963 after some eight months spent languishing in the goods yard at Hove following withdrawal from Brighton shed in December 1962. It was cut up during w/e 21 September 1963. (JG)

"Agatha", "Fingall" and "Car No 53". Following a spell at Cranmore on the East Somerset Railway, she is now to be found working at the Bluebell Railway. Parts of the "Schools" were to live on for some time in the form of snow plough tenders. It had been SR policy to attach large snowploughs to the front of 0-6-0 tender engines, particularly Q, 700 and C classes, during the winter months and using two locomotives, coupled tender to tender, so have a formidable snow clearing machine at their disposal. With the phasing out of steam, the need arose for independent ploughs capable of propulsion by diesel locomotives. In 1964/65 Eastleigh Works developed two series of such ploughs, the first using withdrawn "Schools" tenders and the second using mainly ER V2 tenders. Of the eleven "Schools" tenders originally set aside, only eight were actually converted and were given Departmental numbers in the series ADS70201-29. Although swapping of tenders between locomotives had occurred during the years since construction, the tenders so converted originally belonged to Nos 30901/15/23/29/31/33/34/39. Amazingly the last of these ploughs saw service until well into the 1990s, over 30 years since the last of their parent locomotives was withdrawn from service. Most of these tenders have found homes in preservation since withdrawal with, in some cases, a view to adaptation to suit preserved locomotives whose original tenders have

not survived, for example Nos 34072 "257 Squadron", 35010 "Blue Star", S15 30830 and U 31638. Smaller relics, in the form of nameplates, adorn some of the public schools after which the class was named. Following an initiative by Eastbourne College, when they learnt of the imminent scrapping of the "Schools", the nameplate from No 30914 was presented to the school. The BR Public Relations Department realising the publicity value of such a move, followed this up with more presentations such as that to Whitgift School in early 1964. In many cases these plates complemented the official framed photograph, signed by R.E.L. Maunsell, which had been presented to the school upon the introduction of its namesake locomotive.

It is now over 80 years since this famous class was introduced by the Southern Railway and 50 since the last batch was withdrawn. Whilst their twilight years were sad in many ways and their end particularly brutal, we were lucky to have had them for as long as we did. If the SR had electrified the Hastings route after World War II, as originally intended, they may well have gone a lot sooner. Though they are long disappeared from the railway scene, the passage of time has not dimmed the memory of the glory days of what many still consider to be the most handsome 4-4-0 ever to run in these islands.

'SCHOOLS OUT COMPLETELY' - THE FATE OF A CLASS

SCHOOLS CLASS DISPOSALS

ASHFORD WORKS 30900, 30904, 30907, 30909, 30914, 30919, 30920, 30922, 30924, 30931, 30932, 30933, 30938, 30939

EASTLEIGH WORKS
30901, 30903, 30905, 30906, 30908, 30910, 30911, 30912, 30913, 30915, 30916, 30917, 30918, 30923, 30927, 30929, 30930, 30934, 30936, 30937

COHENS, KETTERING
30902, 30921, 30935

PRESERVED
30925 (National Railway Museum), 30926 (North York Moors Railway), 30928 (Bluebell Railway).

Right - No 30900 with its official name chalked on the cylinder and its unofficial title on the backing plate is captured on Brighton shed. (Ian Nolan)

In a seasonal snow flurry doyen of the class No 30900 "Eton", once considered as a candidate for preservation, awaits the end at Ashford Works which despatched 14 members of the class. Two of the "Schools" scrapped at Ashford, 30922 and 30931, together with seven other Southern locomotives, were dismembered into large pieces and travelled to Swinton near Rotherham in November 1961 for final cutting. In 1962 No. 30900 was reported as being stored unserviceable at Brighton shed in dilapidated condition - the missing front cylinder cover will be noted - could this have been the reason for the 'unserviceable' term and subsequent withdrawal? It was destined to remain at Brighton for over a year. Whilst lying derelict at Brighton it had its nameplates removed and by June 1961 a scrolled inscription 'Borstal' had been substituted on the backing plate either by a disaffected railwayman or some enthusiast wag. (JG)

No 30915 "Brighton" seen at Eastleigh Works in August 1963 during its 5 month sojourn here from July 1963 until scrapping in November of that year. It had also spent time stored in Hove Goods yard along with classmates 30901, 30911, 30916 and 30923. 20 of the class met their end at Eastleigh. (JG)

DEMISE OF THE 'SCHOOLS' CLASS

Withdrawn	No	Name	Scrapped	
February 1961	30919	Harrow	Ashford	3/61
	30932	Blundells	Ashford	8/61
June 1961	30939	Leatherhead	Ashford	9/61
July 1961	30904	Lancing	Ashford	9/61
	30914	Eastbourne	Ashford	9/61
	30938	St Olave's	Ashford	9/61
September 1961	30907	Dulwich	Ashford	9/61
	30908	Westminster	Eastleigh	10/61
	30931	King's Wimbledon	Ashford	11/61
October 1961	30918	Hurstpierpoint	Eastleigh	11/61
December 1961	30905	Tonbridge	Eastleigh	2/62
	30910	Merchant Taylors	Eastleigh	1/62
	30920	Rugby	Ashford	1/62
	30922	Marlborough	Ashford	1/62
	30933	King's Canterbury	Ashford	12/61
January 1962	30913	Christ's Hospital	Eastleigh	2/62
	30924	Haileybury	Ashford	1/62
	30927	Clifton	Eastleigh	3/62
February 1962	30900	Eton	Ashford	3/62
	30909	St Paul's	Ashford	3/62
November 1962	30912	Downside	Eastleigh	1/63
	30917	Ardingly	Eastleigh	4/63
	30928	Stowe	Preserved	
December 1962	30901	Winchester	Eastleigh	8/63
	30902	Wellington	Cohens	4/64
	30903	Charterhouse	Eastleigh	3/64
	30906	Sherborne	Eastleigh	4/63
	30911	Dover	Eastleigh	9/63

'SCHOOLS OUT COMPLETELY' - THE FATE OF A CLASS

30915	Brighton	Eastleigh	10/63
30916	Whitgift	Eastleigh	9/63
30921	Shrewsbury	Cohens	4/63
30923	Bradfield**	Eastleigh	8/63
30925	Cheltenham	Preserved	
30926	Repton	Preserved	
30929	Malvern	Eastleigh	3/63
30930	Radley	Eastleigh	5/64
30934	St Lawrence*	Eastleigh	8/63
30935	Sevenoaks	Cohens	4/64
30936	Cranleigh	Eastleigh	10/63
30937	Epsom	Eastleigh	6/63

** Originally named "Uppingham" but permission was refused by the Headmaster. One of the original plates is still held in Uppingham School.

* Briefly swapped plates with" Westminster" in March 1938 for the French President's special train to avoid offending sensibilities regarding the loss of Quebec to the British above the waters of the St Lawrence river.

A memory of the last year of service of these fine locomotives - one of the railtours powered by a Schools during 1962 was on 13 May when the RCTS "East Midlander" railtour, seen here at Nottingham Victoria, ran with No 30925 "Cheltenham" coupled ahead of 2P No 40646. No 30925 was chosen by the BRB to represent the class in the National Collection given that not only was 30900 in such a bad state, having been stored for many months in the open at Brighton shed, but it was also not in original condition, having been fitted with a multiple jet blastpipe.(JG)

No 30934 "St Lawrence" captured at Eastleigh in late 1962 shortly before it went into storage at Basingstoke for six months. It subsequently proved to be the last Schools to move under its own steam when, towing a dead Drummond 700 Class No 30368, it travelled from Basingstoke to Eastleigh on 18 May 1963 for scrapping in August. (JG)

Opposite top - SE&CR Wainwright D1 class 4-4-0 No 31487 was built in July 1902 by Ashford / Beyer Peacock, it was withdrawn from Bricklayers Arms MPD in February 1961 and scrapped at Ashford Works in April 1961. The loco is carrying a 73B Bricklayers Arms shedcode plate, the depot closing in June 1962. The loco is standing in the scrap line at Ashford Works, during an RCTS visit on Sunday 19 March 1961. Photographer unknown, but possibly E.A.S. Cotton (Geoff Plumb)

Opposite bottom - Maunsell L1 class 4-4-0 No 31782 was built in April 1926, as North British No 23363, it was withdrawn in February 1961 from 70A Nine Elms MPD and scrapped at Ashford Works in May 1961. It is carrying a 74A shedcode plate - Ashford MPD - but this changed to 73F in October 1958. The loco is facing "Schools" class 4-4-0 No 30933 "King's Canterbury" and is ahead of D1 class 4-4-0 No 31487. Date as previous caption. Photographer unknown, but possibly E.A.S. Cotton. (Geoff Plumb)

This page, top - No 34032 "Camelford", with rods removed, seen at Nine Elms in March 1967. The locomotive had been withdrawn the previous October and in the left background can be seen the visiting LNER locomotive "The Great Marquess" which operated a railtour on the Southern Region on 12 March 1967. (JG)

This page, centre - No 35007 "Aberdeen Commonwealth" one of the Bulleids remaining at Nine Elms on the very last day that Nine Elms was technically "open" 26 August 1967. (Jonathan Martin)

This page, bottom - Not only have the connecting rods been removed, which can be seen lying on the ground but the chimney of this Ivatt tank, No 41284 seen at Nine Elms following withdrawal in March 1967, has also been removed possibly as a spare, although this is unlikely at this late date. A more probable explanation is perhaps as a safety measure for its journey to the scrapyard. (JG)

Top - U class Mogul No 31627 lies withdrawn at Eastleigh, 6 November 1965. Note the wooden chock in the slidebar to prevent piston movement. (Geoff Plumb)

Bottom - No 30582 still showing signs of how it had been 'spruced-up' for railtour duty around south-west London on 19 March 1961. (Geoff Plumb)

Opposite top - LSWR Adams "Radial Tank" 4-4-2T class 0415 No 30584 sits dumped at Eastleigh depot after withdrawal from service. Three locos of the class survived to work the Lyme Regis branch but finally succumbed to progress. This loco and No 30582 were scrapped, but No 30583 was preserved on the Bluebell Railway. Alongside is "Lord Nelson" class 4-6-0 No. No 30855 "Robert Blake", also awaiting its fate. No 30584 was built by Dubs in 1885, works number 2109, and was withdrawn from Exmouth Junction shed in February 1961. It was scrapped at Eastleigh Works in December 1961. No 30855 was built at Eastleigh Works in 1928 and was withdrawn from Eastleigh shed in September 1961, also being scrapped at Eastleigh in February 1962. Date of this view uncertain, but most probably a winter afternoon in 1961. (Geoff Plumb)

Bottom right - LSWR B4 Class 0-4-0T No 30102 was one of the engines used in the docks in Southampton and also for shunting at Winchester City but has now sadly reached the scrap line at Eastleigh, sandwiched between two A1X "Terrier Tank" 0-6-0Ts Nos 32662 and 32650 on Saturday 9 May 1964. Happily, all three of these engines were bought for preservation and survive to this day. (Geoff Plumb)

Opposite top - Ex-LB&SCR "Terrier" Class A1X 0-6-0T No 32662 has reached the scraproad at Eastleigh MPD along with several other engines, including B4 Class 0-4-0T No 30102 behind and an unidentified tender engine in front. Saturday 9 May 1964. (Geoff Plumb)

Opposite bottom - On the scrap road at Eastleigh MPD a couple of young spotters have just "cabbed" B4 Class 0-4-0T No 30102 which is surrounded by "Terrier" 0-6-0Ts of Class A1X. On the left is No 32662, the main subject is 32650 while on the right is No 32646. Saturday 9 May 1964. (Geoff Plumb)

This page, top - Former River class tank engine but seen here as rebuilt into U class 2-6-0 No 31800. (Geoff Plumb)

This page, bottom - No 33018 Eastleigh shed. Withdrawn in July 1965 this Q1 spent several months in store at Nine Elms before despatch to Cashmore's of Newport. (Nigel Kendall)

Top left - SR Maunsell Class Q 0-6-0 No 30548 is out of use at Eastleigh MPD together with a Bulleid Q1 on the left and a BR Standard 4MT 2-6-0 on the right, Saturday 9 May 1964.

This page, centre - SR Urie S15 Class 4-6-0 No 30512 sits on the scrapline at Eastleigh MPD, though it was one of the lucky ones that survived into preservation. Behind is an unidentified unrebuilt Bulleid Pacific, its nameplate removed and coat of arms crudely cut out from its air-smoothed casing. Saturday 9 May 1964.

Opposite top - W24 'Calbourne' (now preserved) passes withdrawn No W32 'Bonchurch' near Brading. 19 July 1965.

Opposite bottom O2 class 0-4-4T No W32 "Bonchurch" sits dumped in the siding south of Brading station, rusting and shorn of its nameplates. It had been withdrawn from service in September 1964 and is gradually being reclaimed by nature. Monday 19 July 1965.

This page , bottom - N class 2-6-0 No 31811 Eastleigh 25 July 1965.

(Images both pages Geoff Plumb)

Opposite top - Taken on the last day of steam on the IOW, 31 December 1966, the four 02s in view on shed were Nos W24 'Calbourne', W31 'Chale', W22 'Brading' and W16 'Ventnor'. W24 and W31 had just worked their last train, the LCGB Isle of Wight Steam Farewell Railtour. The train seen passing in the distance is the 15.45 Ryde to Shanklin service headed by No W27 'Merstone', the last 02 to work a BR passenger train on the island. (George Woods)

Opposite bottom - O2 No 35 "Freshwater" at Ryde St John's shed in 1966. (JG)

Right - Its glory days behind it No 35030 'Elder Dempster Lines' awaits the end at Salisbury dump. (Railphotoprints)

Bottom - No 34076 at Salisbury MPD 14 August 1966. "41 Squadron" stayed here for ten months after withdrawal in January 1966 until towed away to Cashmore's. (George Woods)

Above - One of the few Ivatt tanks to be stored at Salisbury dump was No 41319, seen here on 25 February 1968 shortly before its final journey. (JG)

Middle - With some parts already removed, No 30860 'Lord Hawke' in the process of being scrapped at the rear of Eastleigh Works in the summer of 1962. Ironically retained boilers newly coated with red oxide primer lie to the right. (Nigel Kendall)

Bottom - 18 February 1962 sees H15 classmates Nos 30476 and 30475 awaiting the end at Eastleigh. Among the last to be withdrawn, at the end of 1961, this pair met their fate in March 1962. (JG)

Opposite page - Original Bulleid "West Country" Class 4-6-2 No. 34035 "Shaftesbury" looks as though it has reached the end of the line on the scrap road at Eastleigh Works. Already shorn of nameplates and smokebox numberplate it will soon join its unidentified classmate behind, in a rather more advanced state of dismantling. November 1963. Photo by Mike Burnett. (Geoff Plumb)

Top - A Bulleid and a Standard Class 4 No 75079 at Westbury sidings on 30 March 1967 en route to South Wales (JG)

Bottom - No 80083 and a Standard tank classmate parked in Westbury sidings en route to South Wales 29 October 1966. 'Abergavenny' is chalked on the sidetank reflecting the name formerly adorning one of the former LBSCR 'Baltic' tanks. (JG)

Top - No 34056, still with "Croydon" nameplates attached, hauls condemned locos through Bath from Eastleigh including Nos 76017, 82016, 31401, and 35021, 11 October 1965. No 76017 was subsequently rescued and now resides on the Mid-Hants railway.

This page, centre and bottom - Whilst Warship D847 "Strongbow" was taking Q1s Nos 33027 and 33020 and standard tank No 84014 from Eastleigh to South Wales on 2 April 1966, No 33020 developed a hot box and was put off at Bath Goods where it stayed for a week. (A strict speed limit applied to the movement of dead engines - usually 25 mph. This was necessary due to wear and possible poor lubrication to the journals, whilst in addition driving wheels no longer connected by coupling rods were therefore out of balance with each other and consequential hammer-blow on the track was increased.) The reduced length train then continued behind the same diesel hauling Nos 33027, 84014 and brake van. Is this smoke from the hot box hanging around the wheels? (All Derek Fear)

Left - Having been removed from a convoy of scrap locos en route to South Wales, West Country Pacific No 34002 "Salisbury" sits in Bath Westmoreland Goods Yard awaiting further movement to Cashmore's Yard in Newport. It should be noted that the SR roundel and number have been chalked on the front of the locomotive, albeit incorrectly. (www.railphotoprints.co.uk - John Chalcraft)

Opposite page - Rebuilt West Country Pacific No 34013 "Okehampton" recessed at Bath Westmoreland Yard (in the company of No 34100 "Appledore") while en route from Salisbury to Cashmore's Newport, September 1967. The two locos were moved to Bristol Bath Road Depot for exhibition at the Open Day before continuing their journey. (www.railphotoprints.co.uk - John Chalcraft)

April 1967, rebuilt West Country Pacific No 34026 "Yes Tor" stands in Bath Westmoreland Goods yard having been dropped from one of the Salisbury - South Wales scrap trains due to a hot box, its journey to Buttigieg's Yard in Newport was completed in May 1967, but the loco was not cut up until October 1967. (www.railphotoprints.co.uk - John Chalcraft)

Opposite top - No 34052 "Lord Dowding" at Gloucester Horton Road Depot in late 1967 en route to South Wales in the company of a Bulleid classmate and a Standard. (David J Smith)

Opposite bottom - No 73093 stops over at Gloucester Horton Road en route to Cashmore's. (David J Smith)

Right - No 34002 "Salisbury" at Gloucester Horton Road shed where it received the attention of enthusiasts prior to its final journey to South Wales. (David J Smith)

Bottom - No 76015 seen at Severn Tunnel Junction 14 May 1966. (George Woods)

No 30902 "Wellington" amid the debris of Cohen's yard, Kettering is prepared for the final onslaught, already the tender raves have been removed on one side. A sad end for the most powerful 4-4-0s to grace BR metals. (JG)

Left - No 34098 'Templecombe' seen awaiting entry to Buttigieg's yard Newport in October 1967. (JG)

Opposite top - On a depressing day which seems to match the sad appearance of the engine, No 35030 "Elder Dempster Lines" is seen at Buttigieg's Newport in September 1968. (Railphotoprints)

Opposite bottom - Mo 35008 "Orient Line" at Buttigieg's Newport awaiting scrapping in early 1968. Behind the cab are the mortal remains of classmate No 35023. (JG)

No 34060
"25 Squadron" at
Cashmore's Yard
Newport, in the
summer of 1968. The
associated engine
record card is
beneath. (JG)

§PS (11/46) **S.R.** Engine No. *34060* Class *B of B* (PS 833)

IN	OUT	TEN-DER	BOILER		CYLINDERS		BLAST PIPE	LAGGING	CHARGE HAND	REMARKS
			Number	Pressure	Diameter L.	R.				
29/3/56	31/3/56	3287	1341	250	16.712 16.538	16.68	Part refit		G Hobbes W Wright Kasper	Porter Injectors Feed gear. Blr mountin Stm pipe gland Vac ejectr
16/4/56	27/4/56								Kasper	R L Coupled A 'Box
28/10/57	27/11/57	3287	1341	250	16.800 16.312 16.		Refit		G Hobbes Kilpin Forrest	W/box a Brgs. Drag gear Sprg gear Brake Gear Injection By Valve
1 5/59	30 6/59	3287	1341	250	— L & R 16.835 RE 16.620	16.730	Part Refit	—	G. HOBBS. W. FORREST A. KILPIN	4/Itter. A'boxes worn drawgear worn. Brake gear and reversing gear worn
11 10/60	26 11/60	3287	1346	250	Chg NEW INS 16.345 MOD OUT 16.231	16.864	Refit Idaglass		E Hobbs A. KASPER L ROBERTS	CONVERSION Speedo Fitted.
16 8/62	8 9/62	3287	1346	250	SOUND 16.392 B D 16.140	16.871	Refit	—	G. HOBBS. W Forrest W MERRYMAN H Lethbridge	4/Inter. Spring Sand & Bke Gear. Inter. D' Gear.
18 8/64	10 10/64	3287	1346	250	— SOUND 16.450 B D 16.745	16.848	Refit	—	A. EVANS W MERRYMAN	LI Inter. Axle boxes Sand and Bke Gear. Hoppers & Ashpan.

IN	OUT	TEN-DER	BOILER		CYLINDERS		BLAST PIPE	LAGGING	CHARGE HAND	REMARKS
			Number	Pressure	Diameter L.	R.				
5/6/66	1/7/66	3287	1346	250	✓ ✓	✓	✓	✓	H. LETHBRIDGE N T ABon	4/CASUAL Tender Typres wolen
									ENGINE WITHDRAWN 9/7/67	

Wagon wheels litter the foreground at Barry where Nos 34070 "Manston" and 34046 "Braunton" await eventual rescue and restoration. (JG)

Right - Urie S15 No 30499 (now privately preserved) is seen at Woodham's yard at Barry. (JG)

Opposite top - A very weather-beaten S15 No 30841 at Barry. This locomotive went on to life in preservation on the Stour Valley Railway followed by a period of main line running as "Greene King". It is currently with the NYMR. (JG)

Opposite bottom - No 31618 was an early departure from Woodham's yard for preservation being the second locomotive to leave Barry, a journey by rail which occurred in January 1969. It is currently on static display at the Bluebell Railway. (JG)

Above - No 34067 "Tangmere" reaches its nadir during its 16-year sojourn at Barry. (JG)

Left - No 35018, 'British India Line' showing the effects of exposure to salt–laden air at Barry. The thin sheet metal of the cab and boiler cladding being most affected. Rescued and undergoing slow overhaul, this particular Merchant Navy has yet to steam again in preservation. (JG)

Bottom - Although there are a number of U's preserved, No 31874 is the only N Class to have escaped the scrapman. (JG)

Opposite - In spite of appearances an incredibly rusty No 34028 "Eddystone" will defy the odds and return to steam. Purchased from Barry for £6,000 in 1984, it was eventually restored to running condition in 2003. (JG)

Nos 34046 'Braunton' and D6122 at Barry. Hard to imagine No 34046 would be rescued and lovingly restored. (JG)

8. In Store at Fratton

The transfer of steam from their traditional South Eastern haunts to the SR's South Western Division resulted from the Kent Coast Electrification of June 1959. One of the classes affected was Maunsell's L1s, the last survivor of which had a somewhat charmed life lingering on half forgotten in Fratton roundhouse until March 1963 before being scrapped at Eastleigh the following month, more than a year after the last of its classmates had met a similar fate. This and other locomotives stored at Fratton are recalled here.

Following Phase I of the Kent Coast Electrification in the summer of 1959, many locomotives found themselves without regular work on the Southern Region's South Eastern Division and attempts were made elsewhere in the region to find them gainful employment. This proved to be no more than a stopgap measure, delaying by a few months or a couple of years at most, the inevitable withdrawal from traffic. This was indeed the scenario that befell Maunsell's L1 4-4-0s which had been introduced in 1926. In early 1959 the allocation of these locomotives had been as follows :-

Dover	31753/54/55/88/89
Ashford	31756/57/58/59/82
Bricklayer's Arms	31783/84
Faversham	31785/86/87

Following electrification of the first phase of the Kent Coast lines one member of the class, 31755, was immediately condemned and sent off to Ashford Works, where it was scrapped in September with a

further example, No 31758, being despatched in October. As there was no pressing need for the services of the remaining thirteen 33 year-old 4-4-0s, especially when there was an embarrassing surplus of the much more powerful "Schools" Class to hand, a couple were put into store in, of all places, the Boiler Shop of Brighton Works. Here Nos 31759 and 31782 found themselves in the company of C Class 31242 and a trio of L Class 4-4-0s Nos 31764, 31765 and 31780. Storage was also to be the lot of No 31757 from July 1960, but at Fratton shed, coded 70F. However, No 31757 was not to be officially withdrawn from stock until December 1961 posing the question, was it ever intended as a candidate for preservation? The decision to send this locomotive as far west as this oddly enough led to it becoming the last extant example of the class as late as 1963. The remaining ten L1s were transferred to Nine Elms, at least on paper if not in reality.

Shortly before Christmas 1960 C Class No 31242 and L1s Nos 31759 and 31782 were exhumed from the stygian gloom of the Brighton Works Boiler Shop and exposed to the light of day in the Works siding near the signal box. It is believed that their use on holiday extra parcels trains was contemplated, it being traditional practice to bring elderly locomotives out of store for this purpose. However, in the event the idea was not proceeded with and they never worked again, the brace of L1s being despatched to Ashford Works in February 1961. On 20 February a visitor to Ashford noted Nos 31759/82/87 on the scrapline awaiting their fate although No 31759 was not officially withdrawn until November that year.

With sacking over the chimney, No 31757 is seen on 14 October 1962 inside the roundhouse at Fratton during its 2½ year sojourn here. (JG)

Z Class 0-8-0 is clearly having some work done on the motion within the roundhouse at Fratton. Sadly it was decided that this design would not be preserved and in 1965 it was sent for scrap. (JG)

By the beginning of 1962, the sole surviving L Class No 31768 together with L1 31786 represented the only former South Eastern 4-4-0s left in traffic. With the withdrawal of these, the last inside cylinder 4-4-0s on the SR would be gone except for the preserved T9 "Greyhound" No.No 120. No 31768 was duly sentenced in w/e 4 January 1962 with No 31786 following in w/e 5 March, the L1 having an impressive final mileage of 1,068,774 miles to its credit. This was not quite the end of the story however, for there still lingered, all but forgotten in the depths of Fratton roundhouse, No 31757. This L1 still sported a 74A (Ashford) shedcode and was to be seen in company with King Arthur No 30777 "Sir Lamiel" which had been withdrawn in October 1961 and earmarked for preservation. Continued storage at Fratton for such a long period was presumably a reflection of the lack of space at Eastleigh, which at that time was still cutting up locomotives, the SR not enlisting the help of outside scrap merchants in earnest until 1964. You might have thought that the somewhat charmed life of this last survivor into 1963 might have led to its

ultimate preservation either by BR or by enthusiasts. But the latter's attention was elsewhere at the time and I cannot recall seeing any attempts being made in the railway press to launch an appeal to save one of these handsome machines. Thus it was, in w/e 23 March 1963, that the last of Maunsell's L1s met its end at Eastleigh Works.

Fratton went on to play host to other locomotives more fortunately set aside for ultimate preservation and in the summer of 1963 the following were noted in the relative security of the roundhouse - A1X No 32662, M7 No 30245, 0298 No 30587, No 30850 "Lord Nelson", No 30925 "Cheltenham" and No 30926 "Repton". Another Fratton resident was to be one of the Z 0-8-0s which rather surprisingly had been provisionally set aside by BR to be part of the National Collection upon withdrawal in late 1962. After storage at Exmouth Junction shed No 30952 was chosen as the best remaining example of the class and arrived at Fratton shed in the summer of 1963 where it was noted in January 1964 in company with the aforementioned preservation candidates as well as T9

No 120 and Maunsell Q No 30538. In the event both the Z and the Q were scrapped, sharing the fate of the last L1. Even though No 30952 was noted at Severn Tunnel Junction en route to a South Wales scrapyard as late as January 1965, the opportunity to save the Z was lost, not that such a beast would have proved particularly useful on fledgling preserved lines.

Following closure of the Hayling island branch in November 1963, a couple of AIX Terriers, which had featured in the last weekend's operations, were briefly stored at Fratton until early January 1964 when No 32662 was steamed again to tow classmate No 32636 up to Eastleigh, both locomotives subsequently being preserved. Fratton was one of the many dumping grounds that the SR used to accommodate the logjam of withdrawn locomotives awaiting scrapping that built up, due to the inability of Eastleigh to meet increasing scrapping demands. A number of locomotives from a variety of classes spent varying amounts of time at the depot before meeting their fate at the hands of the scrapman. Many of these came from Guildford shed where space was at a premium. Details of these are shown overleaf. Commencing in the summer of 1964 these were gradually moved to scrapyards, generally in South Wales. The last movement was on 27 October 1965 when M7 No 30133 formed part of the

21.05 Fratton – Eastleigh freight. The following day it continued its journey to Stoke Gifford on the 06.10 freight service from Eastleigh, meeting its end in Cashmore's yard at Newport the following month.

In 1964 the depot also played host to Bulleid Pacifics working on the Brighton – Plymouth through train during that strange episode when, from 6 January, the 11.30 departure time of the Plymouth service from Brighton was advanced to 11.00 because the train was diverted to run via Portsmouth to eliminate the need for a separate portion from Portsmouth to Fareham. Bulleid Co-Co electric locomotives took over the Brighton – Portsmouth section with the Exmouth Junction Pacific, which formerly ran through to Brighton, now travelling only as far as Portsmouth, stabling overnight at Fratton depot. This bizarre arrangement lasted only until the start of the summer timetable in 1964, when the train was no longer scheduled to run via Portsmouth and diesel traction replaced electric traction from Brighton right through to Salisbury with a separate Portsmouth – Fareham service being reintroduced.

Strangely Tri-ang Railways brought out a green liveried "OO" version of an L1 in the guise of none other than No 31757 itself, a somewhat strange choice

No 31819 with sacking over its chimney (indicating an engine in store) awaits its fate at Fratton seen on 18 April 1964 behind the tender of one of the two Q1s also stored there at this time. It is not known why the smoke deflectors were removed. (JG)

No 30850 "Lord Nelson" was one of a handful of SR locomotives preserved for the national collection and spent some time at Fratton where it is seen outside the shed with motion removed. (JG)

given the much greater popularity of other classes not at that time represented amongst the ranks of "OO" models. I did buy one of these models, which went out of production in 1967, but I felt it was always rather underpowered and gave problems running over points with only 4-coupled wheels from which to pick up the current. Nonetheless the full size version of these 4-4-0s had given sterling service for more than 30 years, with perhaps their most successful periods being on expresses to Folkestone and Hastings, the Charing Cross - Dover Pullman Car train, and double heading with other 4-4-0s and latterly with Bulleid Pacifics on the "Night Ferry" service right from inception in 1936 until the end of steam on this route in 1959.

By 1966 Fratton depot had become roofless but was still used for stabling locomotives working into Portsmouth, Bulleid Pacific 34088 being noted here in steam on 23 October. Indeed steam servicing facilities remained available to the declining number of visiting locomotives until the very end of SR steam in July 1967. By early 1969 the main depot had been demolished, except for the part used as offices, as had the water tower and the buildings

SR locomotives subsequently sent for scrapping following storage at Fratton 1963 - 1965

Class	No	From	To
Q	30538	7/63	6/64
Q1	33022	1/64	7/64
	33034	1/64	5/64
M7	30133	8/65	10/65
Z	30952	7/63	9/64
N	31819	1/64	6/64
U	31618	1/64	5/64 +
	31625	1/64	5/64 #
	31638	1/64	5/64 +
	31806	1/64	5/64 #

+ Rescued from Barry Scrapyard for preservation on the Bluebell Railway.
# Rescued from Barry Scrapyard for preservation on the Mid Hants Railway.

constructed in 1947 to house the oil pumps for the ill-fated oil burning locomotive trials. Thus ended the history of Fratton, the only complete roundhouse on the Southern Region, which had been constructed back in 1891, being used jointly by the LSWR and the LBSCR from the outset until the grouping in 1923. There was much fierce rivalry between the two companies, even the roads within the roundhouse being strictly allocated between the two companies. As

the years progressed, much larger steam locomotives were introduced, which meant that the 50ft turntable could not accommodate all types resulting in a triangle of lines being constructed in the vicinity so that larger engines could be turned. The depot is perhaps best remembered in later years as the stabling point for the Hayling Island Terriers but it did undertake a fascinating role in the storage both of redundant and preservation stock towards the end of steam.

Above - With motions removed No 30777 "Sir Lamiel" and 30850 "Lord Nelson" were captured at Fratton in 1963. (JG)

Right - Restored T9 No. No 120 in Fratton roundhouse (JG)

9. The Final Journey

It was at the sheds or storage points that portable equipment such as lamps, shovels, fire irons and potentially hazardous items such as the engine's stock of detonators was removed. Tenders were emptied of coal, connecting rods taken off and sometimes thrust unceremoniously into firebox doors. Valve gear linkages were partly dismantled and tied up with rope in preparation for their onward journeys. Movement of dead engines was governed by "Special Notices" which specified the exact running of the train, where and when stops were to be made for examination, primarily for "hot box" detection, together with maximum running speed. Typically halts were made, where convenient, every 25 miles or so and the train, which was classed as an "Out of Gauge Load", was restricted to a maximum running speed of 25 mph. A small tag would be tied to the locomotive's handrail recording the purchaser and destination. If a brake van was not provided then the provision of a "rider" for one or more of the locomotives was deemed necessary whose job it was to operate the engine's handbrake to give additional braking power when required. Vacuum braked wagons might also be included in the train again to provide additional braking power, the maximum load permitted for a dead engine movement being four locomotives.

Top - No 34006 "Bude" parked in a siding at the east end of Salisbury station in July 1967 awaiting the final journey. A far cry from the Locomotive Exchange Trials of 1948 when it represented SR pacific power. (JG)

Bottom - A standard class 5 and a WC, possibly Nos 34012 "Launceston" and 73113, seek temporary refuge in a siding near Warblington Halt just outside Havant. (JG)

Opposite top - A quartet of Standards at Eastleigh having been prepared for the tow to the scrapyard. (JG)

Opposite bottom - Originally destined for the Isle of Wight to replace the ageing O2s, a change of heart saw No 84014 in a convoy of three locomotives approaching Bath Goods Yard where one of their number, Q1 No 33020 with a hot box, was to be put off - see page 59. (Derek Fear)

Examples of Dead Engine movements reported in the railway press

Movements of withdrawn locomotives was a regular feature of the Railway Observer reports for the period. The following extracts give a flavour of the variety and frequency of movements together with some of the pitfalls inherent in moving "dead stock".

1964

"At the end of February the total number of engines dumped or in store on the SR was 116. It was reported that there had been a steady reduction in all regions thanks to the efforts of scrap contractors. A determined effort was being made to clear the dump of remaining Moguls at Stewarts Lane, many of which were destined for King's of Norwich."

Processions of dead engines en route to South Wales are a regular occurrence, all have to be routed via Gloucester as they are not allowed through the Severn Tunnel. On 16 June 31618 was noted at Bristol towing a string of SR engines. The following day a Q1 was seen towing three of its classmates."

By the time of this view, May 1966, No 84014 had reached Severn Tunnel Junction. (Patrick O'Brien)

Some further reported movements include –

"31613 / 31617 / 31796 / 31810 were en route from Nine Elms to Swansea East Dock on 24 June 1964. 31913 / 31917 / 33010 began their trip from Feltham to Swansea on 25 June 1964. 33024 / 33034 / 31819 from Fratton were noted en route to Swansea on 26 June 1964. All of the above were moved to Bird's of Morriston."

"30021 / 31305 / 31542 / 31551 moved to Briton Ferry on 13, 14, 15, 16, June 1964 respectively. 31551 left in a freight train and on the same day 80141 hauled 31870 / 33014 / 33029 away from Three Bridges. 33014 soon ran hot and was put off at Chichester where it remained for some days but by 21 June 1964 it had been reunited with the other two locomotives in a siding at Warminster. 31618 / 31625 / 31638 / 31806 were taken to Barry on 16 June 1964. 31874 was noted upon arrival at Barry on 7 June 1964."

"On 28 June 1964, 31407 / 31837 / 31870 arrived at the now closed Swansea East Dock shed from Feltham for cutting at Bird's but were still there in late July. Condemned engines are now being moved at frequent intervals from Feltham, Fratton and Nine Elms to

South Wales. Some are moving from Central Division sheds to South Wales via Eastleigh. One such train ran into trouble on 18 June 1964 when 30506 hauling 30499 / 30841/30847 from Feltham to Barry only got as far as Staines Central when assistance had to be summoned from Feltham."

"M7s stored at Eastleigh since withdrawal in May are now being moved to Briton Ferry. They have been hauled from Eastleigh to Salisbury Fisherton Goods as part of the 03.20 Brighton-Salisbury freight. The following movements took place in September - 30107, 30480, 30029, 30057, 30108 and 30667 on the 2, 3, 9, 10,11 and 15 respectively. "

"The preserved locomotives held at Fratton for several months moved on 13 September when a D65xx hauled 30850,30245,30587 to Basingstoke but owing to a hot box on the Beattie the procession only went to Woking the following day. They moved to Stratford later that week. On 20 September 30777, 30925 and T9 120 were moved to Basingstoke, proceeding to Stratford on 21 September."

"Q1 33036 was hauled from Three Bridges to Risca on 26 September. 31868 was noted stored at Gloucester Barnwood in November."

"92003 was observed at Ashley Hill, Bristol on 19

October towing 31812 / 31849 / 31856 up the bank en route to South Wales. 34057 appeared in a siding alongside the Fishponds line outside Bristol Temple Meads, and at nearby Barrow Road shed 30952 and 31406 were noted on Christmas Day."

"On 3 December 31412 / 31814 / 31869 were booked to be hauled from Eastleigh to Warminster. A collection of locomotives had congregated at Salisbury from Eastleigh and Nine Elms during December and on the 7 December 30830 / 34027 / 35006 and 35018 were due to be taken from Salisbury to Barry. On 7 December 34064 was seen heading down the West of England mainline towing 34027 and 35018."

1966

"34005 hauled 34053 / 76068 from Eastleigh as far as Romsey on 11 January 1966 although coupling rods stacked in the tender of 34053 hit some bridges near Chandlers Ford and after some consultation the locomotives were parked in the east siding at Romsey station."

Early in 1966 The Railway Observer reported that as most members of the 84xxx class on LM region are surplus to requirements they are being transferred to the SR for use on the Isle of Wight to replace the ageing Adams tanks. Modifications were to be carried out at Ryde works as engines are being sent direct to Fratton for shipment to the island. 84014, one of the first to arrive on the region, developed a hot box at Basingstoke on 24 October 1965 and had to be stopped on shed. In the event the scheme was dropped in favour of electrification with redundant LT tube stock and 84014 together with its other redundant classmates, was sent for scrapping.

Passing through Gloucester, stock was often stabled at Horton Road shed and during the period 25 October to 10 November the following were noted: 34100 / 34103 / 41312 / 80015 / 80016 / 80085 / 80133 / 80139 / 80143 / 80146 / 80152 / 82019 / 82029."

Withdrawn moguls stored on the east side of the coaling stage at Eastleigh. (Mark Abbott)

No 34071 "601 Squadron" is shunted into position for the final move in company with a USA tank, both devoid of coupling rods to facilitate transport. (JG)

Nos 34100 "Appledore" and 34013 "Okehanpton" were hijacked en route to South Wales for display at a very wet Bath Road Open Day in October 1967. The pair were seen previously at Bath Westmoreland yard, page 61. (JG)

Q class 0-6-0s Nos 30532 and 30538 reverse into Andover pulled by No 73169. In the background, in steam and working, is No 76016. (JG)

Passing Gloucester in August 1967 is a freight bound for South Wales, with three West Country Pacifics and a Standard class 5 in the consist. The locos are - Nos 73119 "Elaine", 34098 "Templecombe", 34108 "Wincanton" and 34104 "Bere Alston". All four locos are bound for Buttigieg's at Newport, where they will be promptly disposed of. (David J Smith)

Right - Z Class No 30952 with motion tied with rope and coupling rod on the tank top waits with No 34105 "Swanage" at Eastleigh in October 1964. (JG)

Bottom - No 30952 parked near Bristol's Barrow Road shed in company with a pannier tank en route to South Wales. (Peter Leigh)

Above - An unidentified 'N' class in charge of two withdrawn N1s leaving Hove station, possibly en route to Eastleigh, 28 June 1963. Note withdrawn locomotives stored on the far right. (Ian Nolan)

Left - The pair of Q 0-6-0s seen previously at Andover Junction (page 84) Nos. 30532 and 30538 were captured on Banbury shed in October 1964 en route to Wards scrapyard of Killamarsh in Derbyshire, who despatched five examples of this particular Maunsell design. (JG)

Opposite page - 23 February 1965 WC pacific No 34051 "Winston Churchill" takes on water at Salisbury while hauling locos 34045 "Ottery St Mary", 34105 "Swanage" and Q class 0-6-0 30541 from Eastleigh to South Wales. The loco hauled the train as far as Westbury. It is an extraordinary coincidence that three of the engines have the same numbers in different combinations. (Nigel Kendall)

SCRAPPING THE SOUTHERN

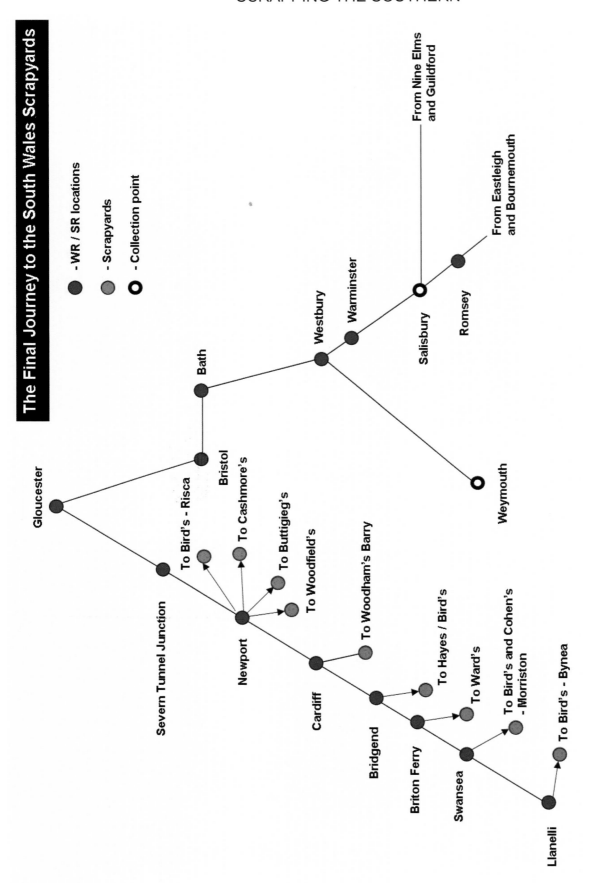

The Final Journey to the South Wales Scrapyards

Above - Q1 Class 0-6-0 No 33004 recessed in the carriage sidings at Bristol Barrow Road while en route to Birds, Morriston, 16 October 1965. (Railphotoprints.co.uk - Mike Jefferies)

Below - Rebuilt Merchant Navy No 35024 "East Asiatic Company" is also seen recessed in the carriage sidings at Bristol Barrow Road while en route to Woodfields, Town Dock, Newport, 16 October 1965. (Railphotoprints.co.uk - Mike Jefferies)

10. Private Scrapyards used by the SR

Some 13 private scrapyards at 18 sites were involved in cutting locomotives from the SR, many were in South Wales but others were to be found as far afield as Yorkshire, Northamptonshire, Essex and Norfolk.

In his book "**Steam for Scrap**", first published in 1985, Nigel Trevenna classifies private scrapyards into four grades with ten locations constituting 'Grade 1' yards, ie those large commercial concerns responsible for cutting hundreds of BR locomotives. In this category are Messrs. Cashmore's of Newport, Bird's of Risca, Ward's of Killamarsh and Buttigieg's of Newport, all of which played their part in scrapping SR stock. The 'Grade 2' yards, of slightly lesser importance but each

of which cut dozens of locomotives, includes Bird's of Morriston, Cohen's of Kettering and of Morriston, King of Norwich, Settle Speakman of Queenborough, Hayes of Bridgend later taken over by Bird's, and Woodham's of Barry. Further down the pecking order but still contributing significant numbers were Bird's of Bynea, Ward's of Briton Ferry and the gloriously named Slag Reduction Co. of Rotherham. The "small fry" yards purchased locomotives in lesser quantities, often in ones and twos, and generally operated for short periods, these included Cox & Danks of Park Royal, Soliffe of Newport Isle of Wight, Ward of Columbia Wharf Grays in Essex, Woodfield of Newport and Thomas Ward of Ringwood.

J Cashmore, Newport Monmouthshire

No 34057 "Biggin Hill" one of the last quartet of "spamcans" in service has arrived at its final destination in this view, taken on 30 September 1967. Traces of whitening, applied when it was working enthusiasts' specials, can still be seen on the front buffers although the smokebox door seems to have lost its fastening and is held shut with rope. Originally subject of an appeal to save the engine, contemporary adverts of the time referred to the choice having moved away from No 34057 commensurate upon its withdrawal. Notice the missing cylinder covers and piston - was this why she had succumbed? (No 34023 was eventually chosen). Withdrawn from Salisbury shed in May 1967, it spent some weeks dead at Nine Elms before returning to Salisbury for a couple of months prior to being towed to South Wales. It was despatched in October 1967. (JG)

Engine record card of No 34057 "Biggin Hill".

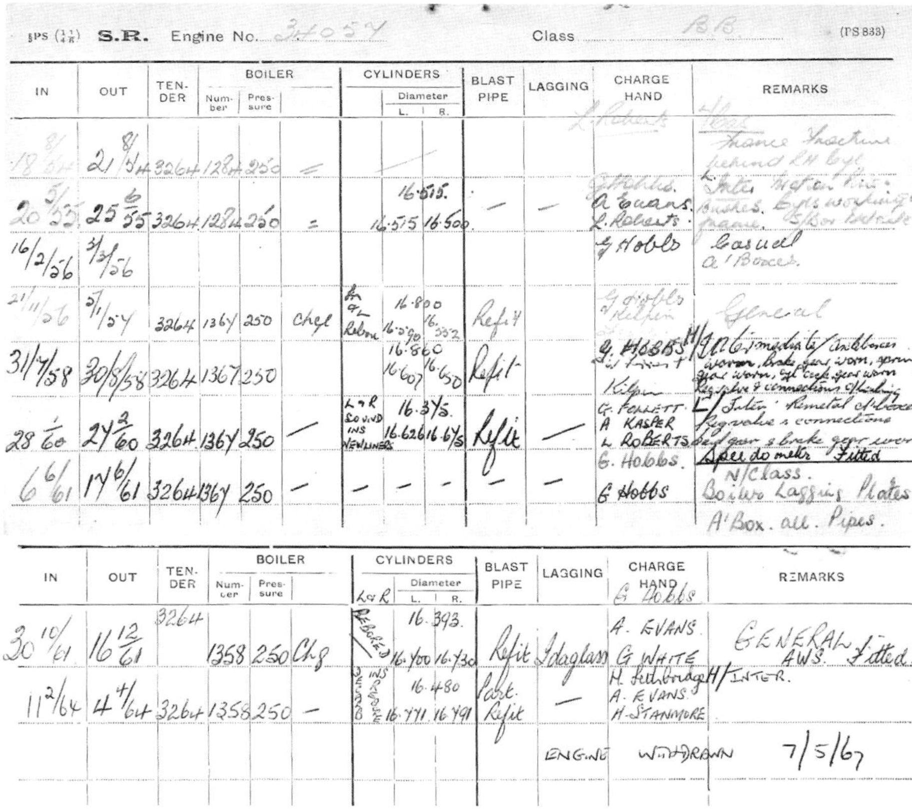

S.R. Engine No. 34057 Class B.B. (PS 833)

IN	OUT	TENDER	BOILER Number	BOILER Pressure	BOILER	CYLINDERS	Diameter L.	Diameter R.	BLAST PIPE	LAGGING	CHARGE HAND	REMARKS
18/8/54	21/8/54	3264	1284	250	=						L. Roberts	Heel Frame fracture behind LH cyl
20/5/55	25/6/55	3264	1284	250	=		16.515. 16.575	16.500.	—	—	G Hobbs. A Evans. L. Roberts.	L. Inter. [illegible] Bushes. Cyls working in frame. S/Box [illegible]
16/2/56	3/3/56										G Hobbs	Casual A'Boxes.
21/11/56	5/1/57	3264	1367	250	Chgd	L & R Rebore	16.800 16.590	16.552	Refit		G Hobbs Kilpin	General
31/7/58	30/8/58	3264	1367	250			16.860 16.607	16.650	Refit		G. HOBBS [illegible] Kilpin	H/I intermediate Axleboxes worn, brake gear worn, spring gear worn, cyl cock gear worn Reg valve & connections [illegible]
28/1/60	24/2/60	3264	1367	250	—	L & R SOUND INS NEW LINERS	16.375. 16.626	16.675	Refit	—	G. FOLLETT. A KASPER L ROBERTS. G. Hobbs.	L/Inter. Remetal A'boxes. Reg valve & connections [illegible] gear & brake gear worn Speedometer Fitted
6/6/61	17/6/61	3264	1367	250	—	—	—	—	—	—	G Hobbs	N/Class. Boiler Lagging Plates. A'Box. all. Pipes.

IN	OUT	TENDER	BOILER Number	BOILER Pressure	BOILER	CYLINDERS L & R	Diameter L.	Diameter R.	BLAST PIPE	LAGGING	CHARGE HAND G Hobbs	REMARKS
30/10/61	16/12/61	3264	1358	250	Chg	REBORED	16.393. 16.400	16.430	Refit	Idaglass	A. EVANS. G WHITE	GENERAL AWS. Fitted.
11/2/64	4/4/64	3264	1358	250	—	INS REBORE	16.480 16.771.	16.791	Part. Refit	—	H. Lethbridge A. EVANS. H-STANMORE	H/INTER.
										ENGINE	WITHDRAWN	7/5/67

More than 40 Bulleid Pacifics were cut up at this yard which could be easily viewed from the adjacent Octopus Bridge. This gave a grandstand view of proceedings, each locomotive being scrapped more or less upon the same spot on one of the sidings. Adjacent to this was the famous scrap pile, a huge mountain of parts sometimes reaching 40 feet in height onto which a large crane dumped an assortment of cylinder blocks, smokeboxes and numerous other parts. Lurking at the bottom of the pile were three Sherman army tanks which were periodically exposed with the ebb and flow of materials. The crane was also used to load hoppers of bite-sized locomotive pieces into lorries.

A visitor to Newport on 13 December 1968 reported that Cashmore's yard was empty whilst at Buttigieg's the last engine present, No 34017, was being cut, having been there for some 18 months. No 34017 "Ilfracombe" therefore had the dubious distinction of being the last of the Bulleid Pacifics to survive at Newport; the previous month the other long term resident of Buttigiegs, No 35030 "Elder Dempster Lines", had met a similar fate.

The famous Cashmore's scrap pile, buried underneath all the locomotive debris were remains of USA Sherman tanks, occasionally revealed when the scrap pile was reduced. (JG)

No 30069 at Cashmore's, 23 March 1967. (John Grey Turner)

J Buttigieg,
Newport Monmouthshire

34005

Opposite, bottom - No 34005 "Barnstaple", first of the rebuilt Bulleids, meets its Waterloo at Buttigieg's yard, October 1967. (David J Smith)

Above - Nos 34103 "Calstock", 34042 "Dorchester" and S15 30833 are seen at Buttigieg's, June 1966. (Patrick O'Brien)

D Woodham, Barry Glamorgan

Locomotives as far as the eye could see, this panorama of the scraplines at Woodhams, Barry was taken in 1967 and features a rebuilt Bulleid on the right and others to right and left in what might be mistaken for a sea of Swindon designs. (JG)

Perhaps the most famous scrapyard of them all, Dai Woodham's yard, became legendary purely because the scrapping of locomotives took second place to the scrapping of vast numbers of wagons. A breathing space was therefore given for enthusiast groups to raise enough funds to purchase ultimately over 200 from them including 41 from the SR. Only four ex-SR locomotives were scrapped here, two S15s, and two Bulleids, Nos 34045 "Ottery St Mary" and 34094 "Mortehoe".

Left - Engine record card for No 34067 "Tangmere" which was rescued from Woodham's yard in January 1981 after spending nearly 16 years rusting away. Coincidentally its service life was also just 16 years from completion in September 1947 to withdrawal in November 1963.

Opposite top - A comparison: a missing tender axle, cab windows and nameplates, but at the time otherwise positively complete, Eastleigh 1964.

Opposite bottom - 34067 'Tangmere' after years of exposure to salt air at Barry with various parts removed yet awaiting what would be a successful rescue and restoration. (JG)

Left - No 31874 at Barry. (JG)

Opposite top - The cutting of Maunsell N Class 2-6-0 No 31851 is well under way at King's Scrapyard, Norwich on 1 August 1964. (Norfolk Railway Society Collection - Roger Harrison)

Opposite, centre left - Nos 31822, 2246, 5205, 31894, 31896 and 31897 are seen in the sidings at Trowse Lower Junction, Norwich awaiting shunting into the nearby King's scrapyard, 18 April 1964. (Norfolk Railway Society Collection - Roger Harrison)

Opposite, centre right - K Class 2-6-0 No 32337 and U1 2-6-0s Nos 31896 and 31894 awaiting scrapping at King's scrapyard, Norwich, 25 April 1964. (Norfolk Railway Society Collection - Roger Harrison)

Opposite bottom - Maunsell N1 2-6-0 No 31822, a long term South Eastern Section performer in Trowse Lower Junction Yard awaiting cutting at King's scrapyard, Norwich, 18 April 1964. This was the only N1 to be cut by a private yard, the others meeting their end at Eastleigh. (Norfolk Railway Society Collection - Roger Harrison)

R Hayes, Bridgend, Glamorgan

On 15 May 1965, three original Bulleids were captured at Hayes scrapyard in Bridgend from a passing train. They were No 34075 nearest the camera with, Nos 34083 and 34062 behind. This yard was taken over by Birds in August of 1965. Six examples of Bulleids were cut up here together with a solitary Maunsell Q Class. (Rail Photoprints)

4P 5FB

31851

Although based in ER territory the yard did not become involved in steam locomotive scrapping until May 1963, by which time the ER had been largely dieselised,so their first purchases came from LMR and WR with SR acquisitions beginning in 1964. When New England shed disposed of A3s Nos 60062 and 60106 along with A1 60129 they began to receive ER steam traction.

Above - Q1 No 33040 in company with an ex LNER A3, of which the yard cut six of the type, 26 October 1964. (Ipswich Transport Museum - H. N. James)

Right - K Class No 32343 at King's of Norwich, 26 October 1964. (Ipswich Transport Museum - H. N. James)

Opposite page - On 7 February 1967 a line up of nine 02s could be seen on the former Freshwater line at Newport, headed by No 27.
The complete line-up was Nos W14/16/17/20/22/27/28/33/35. Later No. 31 was also scrapped here following its retention by BR for engineering trains after the end of scheduled steam services. (John Mackett)

H Soliffe, Newport

Above - Close-up view of No 27, suitably adorned with farewell slogans, receives the attention of a workman who is starting work on cutting the bunker. (John Mackett)

Right - A few days after the other photographs were taken at Newport, scrapped engine and wagon parts are piled high on one of the sidings. They were sad remnants of the Island's Victorian railway. (John Mackett)

Above - Withdrawn No 30923 'Bradfield' being shunted at Brighton by Terrier No 32678, 20 June 1963. (Ian Nolan)

Left - With rods tied up ready for movement - but someone appears to have forgotten the loco lamp - E6 No 32418 stands at Brighton on 7 April 1963. (Ian Nolan)

Top - Shortly after being withdrawn, U1 No 31895 stands at Brighton shed, 23 December 1962. (Ian Nolan recounts, "On a quiet Sunday in the early 1960s, a polite request to the shed foreman could result in a teenager being unofficially allowed to explore the depot discreetly ….".)

Left - On the same December date that No 31895 was recorded, withdrawn K No 32341 awaits its fate at Brighton. All the engines seen here were later reported stored at Hove dump. (Both Ian Nolan)

Top - Hove dump in the winter of 1962 / 1963 as seen from Fonthill Road. Schools Nos 30901 and 30915 stand mantled by snow. A contemporary car and period advertisements add to the charm of the scene. (Ian Nolan)

Left - E4 No 32468 among the line of stored engines at Hove in March 1963. (Ian Nolan)

Right - Three Bridges shed, 24 March 1963. Notwithstanding the missing front bogie, rods and piston / valves, 4MT 2-6-4T No 80140 would live a while longer, being withdrawn in July 1967. Not so fortunate was the 'K', No 32353, which had been withdrawn in December 1962. (Ian Nolan)

Bottom - From the south end of the platform at Three Bridges, a distant view of another withdrawn 'K', this time No. 32345, 21 July 1963. (Ian Nolan)

Seen at the rear of the Eastleigh works during the open day of 9 August 1961 was N15 No 30453. (Ian Nolan)

Adams radial tank No 30584, displaying the varying positions of its cabside number and BR crest which it has carried over the years, is seen at Eastleigh on 14 October 1961, its long reign on the Lyme Regis branch at an end. Lord Nelson No 30858 "Lord Duncan" poses alongside the tank, its career also at an end having been withdrawn a couple of months previously. This had been the first of the trio, which lasted into BR service, to be withdrawn, having amassed a respectable 2,102,781 miles. (Charlie Verrall)

Top - On 7 August 1963, N1 No 31878 has arrived at Eastleigh. (Two other members of the class were in the same line-up) Could this be one of the engines seen leaving Hove on page 86. (Ian Nolan)

Right - Well tank, No 30586, withdrawn in December 1962, alongside the Eastleigh coal stage on 7 August 1963. (Ian Nolan)

Above - End of the road for U1 No 31895, in the middle of a line of three engines at the rear of Eastleigh Works and waiting their turn to be despatched. The date is 7 August 1963. (The others were Nos 30923 and 31901.)

Left - A line up outside the front of Eastleigh works, 29 August 1961. Right is Ivatt, no 41261, not withdrawn but possibly arriving for a works visit - it would survive until July 1965. Next is T9 30313, followed by 700 No 30691, then, M7 30669 and finally another T9 No 30709 All the former LSWR design types had been withdrawn the previous month. (Both Ian Nolan)

Top - 'G6' No 30258 alongside Eastleigh shed, 9 August 1961. This engine had been withdrawn the previous month. The reason for the bottles and other items on the running plate is slightly quizzical - target practice perhaps?

Centre - 'E1' No 32694 in company (behind) with 'C' 31113 at Eastleigh, 9 August 1961, the annual Open Day. Again both engines had been withdrawn in July 1961.

Bottom right - Another 'O2', this time mainland No 30193 photographed on 7 August 1962. Withdrawn in April 1962 it appears to be being used as a form of stationary steam supply.

Bottom left - The remains of 'N', No 31872 in the process of being cut at Eastleigh on 7 August 1963 having been withdrawn in May of the same year. (All Ian Nolan)

Cutting at Eastleigh, 1962-64. This page and overleaf top, Bulleid types being despatched - number details were not recorded. The gantry seen in the view above carried a Rolls-Royce crane used for lifting.

Overleaf bottom - No 30451 'Sir Lamorak' in the early stages of dismantling, 1962.

(Eric Best)

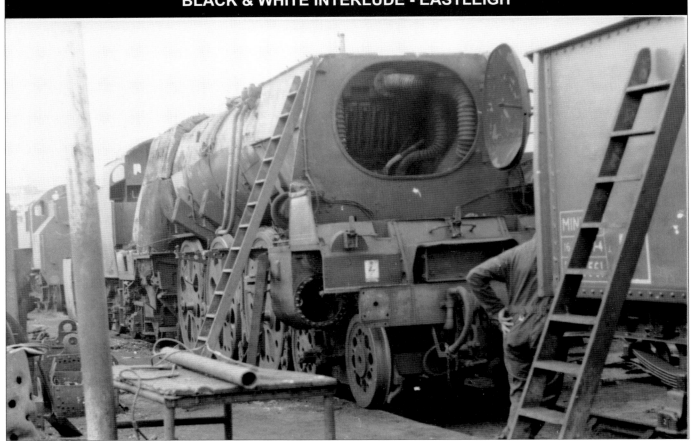

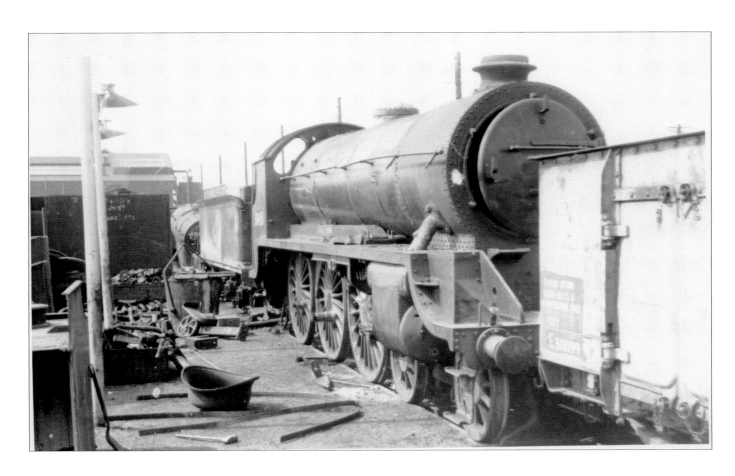

Top - No 33020, seen with a hot box earlier at Bath, has finally reached its destination and is seen at Newport in company with SR diesel shunter No 15202. (Patrick O'Brien)

Bottom - No 76014 ex-Bournemouth at Buttigieg's on 19 January 1967 together with No 9609 ex-Llanelly. The purpose of the rope attached to the smokebox door is unknown (Patrick O'Brien)

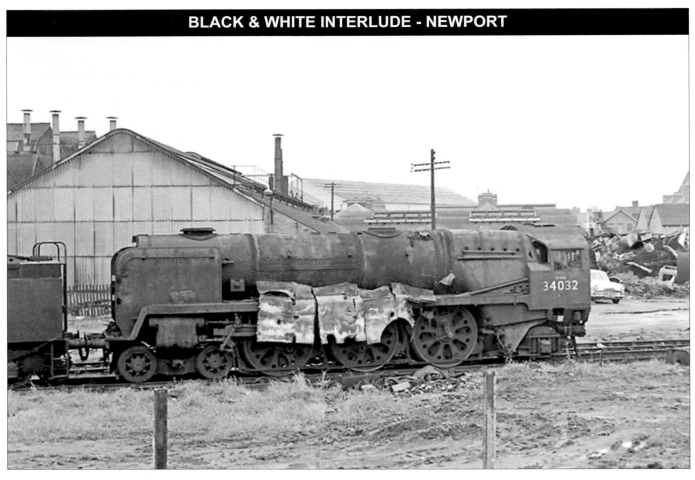

Top - No 34032 'Camelford' at Buttigieg's in September 1967. (David Smith)
Bottom - S15 No 30833, an ex Feltham locomotive, is recorded at Buttigieg's in June 1966. (Patrick O'Brien)

11. A Scrapyard in Detail - Cohen's of Kettering

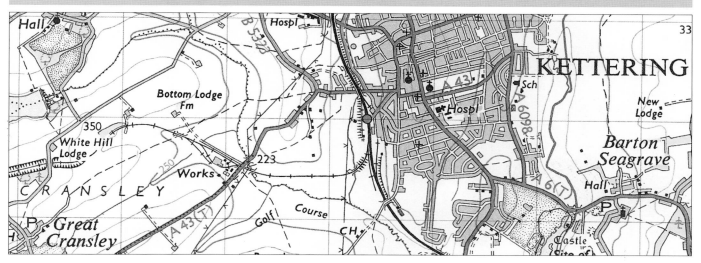

Reproduced from the1960 Ordnance Survey.

Logging on to the "Google Earth" website it is possible to zoom in on the village of Great Cransley, a couple of miles from the town of Kettering in Northamptonshire. Just to the north east of the village beside the main A43 trunk road, is a site now occupied by what looks like a car scrapyard, but which from the early 1960s to 1980 was home to a branch of George Cohen, scrap merchants.

It was in this yard that some unlikely scrapping operations took place, covering a wide variety of surplus railway rolling stock from steam locomotives, of both BR and industrial origin, to London Transport underground cars, plus carriages, wagons and also diesel and electric locomotives. Although steam locomotives from all regions of BR, except Scottish, were to end their days here, perhaps the most unlikely collection was a number of types from the former Southern Region.

The Southern Region of BR was unique in undertaking to rid itself of most unwanted steam locomotives at its own workshops. It was not until early 1964 that the capacity of in-house scrapping facilities became increasingly inadequate with log jams of condemned locomotives cluttering up yards and sidings throughout the region. This led the SR to outsource the scrapping operation to a number of outside contractors who would bid for withdrawn stock in the usual closed tender process. Much of the scrapping was done in South Wales, home of the major players such as Cashmores of Newport, Woodhams of Barry together with Birds of Morriston, Risca, Bynea and Bridgend

and Wards of Briton Ferry. The final locomotive to be scrapped at Eastleigh Works by BR staff is believed to have been Standard tank No 82008, in June 1964.

Although not within the premier league of scrap merchants, as far as BR disposals were concerned, the firm of Cohen's, which also had sites at Morriston near Swansea, Cargo Fleet near Middlesbrough, Coburn Works Tinsley in Sheffield, Rotherwas in Hereford and Kingsbury in Warwickshire, was certainly a major player in accounting for considerable numbers of BR locomotives, 200 steam locomotives being despatched from their Northamptonshire site alone. The Cohen's yard near Kettering, situated on the site of the former Cransley ironstone furnaces, was a mile west of Kettering station, to which it was connected by a single track railway, part of the former Loddington ironstone quarry branch which had closed to regular traffic in June 1963 commensurate with closure of the quarries.

The line was retained for a number of years in the expectation that the quarries might re-open and indeed an RCTS DMU special traversed the branch in May 1968. The special passed Cohens site but as reported in the Railway Observer, *"Advance notice had been given that the party would not be welcome in the scrapyard and a reception party of two men and a dog awaited our arrival. Serious confrontation was however avoided as a shower of rain intervened at the crucial moment. Seventeen BR locomotives were noted in the yard (15 steam and two diesel) as well as 21 tenders, a number of brakevans, and three of Cohen's own locomotives."*

No 30902 "Wellington" awaits its fate in company with ex LT tube stock at Cohen's Kettering yard. (JG)

S15 No 30507 at Cohens, Kettering. The retained smokebox numberplate will be noted. (John Evans)

The actual site was not visible from the mainline but a convenient farm track that led off the A43 ran alongside the full length of the yard affording a grandstand view of proceedings.

Normally it might be expected that scrapyards would be located deep within the urban landscape often surrounded by scenes of dereliction, but illustrations of Cohen's yard at Cransley show the site surrounded by green fields, trees and hedgerows, strangely out of keeping with the scenes of dismemberment of locomotive carcasses that went on there.

Kettering took their first steam locos for scrapping in the spring of 1964, continuing until the supply of steam locomotives dried up post-1968. Scrapping would subsequently continue with diesel and electric types until 1980.

The actual site consisted of sidings on which incoming stock was stored and separate roads on which the actual cutting was done, stock being moved about the site by Cohen's own 0-4-0 diesel shunter "Nellie", although by the end of 1968 this locomotive was out of use and its duties were being performed by former BR diesel D2176.

Most scrap merchants, with of course the notable exception of Woodhams, would deal with stock promptly upon arrival but this was not the case at Cransley, when often several weeks passed before items took their turn on "death row", just two or three locomotives being worked upon at any one time.

Perhaps the record stay of execution was achieved by 2800 Class No 3852, which stood in a siding for over a year before it was scrapped. Additionally locomotives could often be seen in the BR sidings at Kettering awaiting the trip up the spur line to Cransley especially if Cohen's own sidings were fully occupied. Similarly stock would often have taken some time just to arrive at Kettering, either from their home depots or from various BR collection yards. This was not just a reflection of the length of journey involved but also the state of the locomotive in question, for hot boxes or similar ailments would require sidelining or attention en route, thus delaying transit.

A case in point was Maunsell W Class tank No 31924, despatched from London's Nine Elms depot in October 1964 and subsequently noted on Wellingborough shed on 8 November. By the 22 November it had only moved as far as Kettering shed yard, where it was noted alongside ex GWR 72xx 2-8-2T No 7218.

In some cases however, the journey could be interrupted by the attitude of staff operating the relevant freight working, as happened on 27 September 1969 when a trio of Black 5s, en route to Cohens at Kettering were halted at New Mills near Gowhole when the driver reckoned his eight hours duty was up and refused to take the train any further. The consist was consequently parked in the up goods loop. After being left here for more than a month and suffering the attentions of local vandals, the locomotives were pronounced unfit to move until inspected by the C&W Department. Then on 6 December two were moved although the final machine was still there a month later!

Not all movements were long distance, witness the transfer of Ivatt Mogul No 46495 which had spent most of its life allocated to Kettering depot 15B. Locomotives also tended to arrive in batches rather than as singletons. On 1 October 1967 several ex LMS 2-6-4Ts, including Fairburn tank No 42233, were noted in the reception sidings.

Successful tendering meant local enthusiasts were treated to a wide variety of stock and many made regular pilgrimages to the yard to witness the latest arrivals. Perhaps LT 1927 Piccadilly Line Underground stock constituted some of the most bizarre sights to be seen in the Northamptonshire countryside, but equally unusual was the appearance of a number of ex SR classes here. (Details of the SR steam locomotives cut up at Cransley, are given in section 12.)

The end of 1962 had seen withdrawal en bloc of the last members of Maunsell's 4-4-0s, amongst the last of

them being Nos 30902 "Wellington", 30921 "Shrewsbury" and 30935 "Sevenoaks" from Nine Elms depot. They had arrived at Cransley on 24 March 1964 hauled by a Stanier 8F. Previously three S15s Nos 30497 / 30509 / 30514 arrived, towed from Feltham shed on 19 March, whilst the following day a W tank, an H16 and a Q1, Nos 31922 / 30518 / 33002 respectively, also arrived. On 23 March another Q1, No 33013, this time in steam, arrived towing sister engine No 33008 and S15 30507. All were to become local celebrities amongst the railway fraternity, being much photographed in the yard in various stages of demolition. Further Q1s, Nos 33016/33024 and stovepipe chimneyed Q class No 30549 were noted passing Bedford Midland en route to Kettering. These movements, often from the SR collection point at Feltham depot, were operated as Class 8 freights.

At the time, usual practice was for the scrap tonnage to be painted on the locomotives but at Cohen's this was also painted on the tenders where appropriate, S15 No 30507 for example displaying the figures "92T".

The method of scrapping was generally left to the individual gangs concerned, some preferring to start with the cab and working forward whilst others attacked the front end initially, although generally the valuable firebox was left until last. Tenders were often dealt with separately and marshalled with redundant brake vans on a siding leading towards Loddington. At one time it was thought that nothing less than a Merchant Navy might be destined for Cohens, for on 28 September 1964, 8F No 48197 towed in a fresh arrival to Kettering in the shape of No 35002 "Union Castle". However the Merchant was only stopping off on its journey to its ultimate resting place, the Slag Reduction Co of Rotherham where it met its end together with classmate No 35015 "Rotterdam Lloyd".

The Schools were not the only named classes to be handled here, for no less than ten of the ex GWR Grange class met their fate at Cransley, most coming from store at Oxley and Tyseley, although No 6844 "Penhydd Grange" travelled all the way from Llanelly. Other Cohen's sites took a further four Granges.

Kettering took 24 examples of major GWR types including No 5018 "St Mawes Castle" which was hauled by No 73028, almost certainly the first Castle over Midland metals in this area. The only known example of a Hall dealt with at Cransley was 6928 "Underley Hall".

Employees of Cohens also travelled to various locations, including several on the SR, to cut up locomotives deemed unfit to travel, these included Merchant Navy No 35004 "Cunard White Star", Maunsell Moguls Nos 31619 / 31809 / 31866, Q1 No 33015, Standard Class 5 No 73041, Standard tank No 80132, and USA tanks Nos 30066 / 30074, the last two in their departmental guise as Nos DS235/236. These were all dealt with at Eastleigh. Mogul 31850 was cut at Redhill shed. Cohen's "Flying Cutters", as they were known, also dealt with two Standard tanks, Nos 80096 and 80102, on a site at Ringwood in Hampshire. These Flying Cutters were often relatively small teams of dismantlers, for example just three men cut up Nos 31809 / 31866 and 80132 at Eastleigh in the spring of 1966. Other locomotive types previously operating on the SR such as Brighton-based Ivatt tanks Nos 41326 / 41327, five Standard 82xxx tanks from Nine Elms and Standard Class 4 No 76008 from Salisbury, all ended their days at Cransley.

As mentioned previously, the vast majority of ex-SR locomotives not cut up in-house were despatched to the South Wales yards but other players in the disposal story included King's of Norwich who took four N Class, one N1, three U1s, three Ks, one Q, seven Q1s, and one H Class. Wood's at Queenborough saw off one H, one N, two S15s, four Qs, four M7s and four WC/BB Pacifics, whilst Ward's of Grays took three Us, and two members of the Q Class. Cox & Danks cut up a single Q Class at their Park Royal site whilst one U Class travelled north to Slag Reduction of Rotherham, which also dealt with the two Merchant Navy's referred to earlier. Five Qs headed to Ward's of Killamarsh in Sheffield. In summary some 13 firms at 18 sites were involved in scrapping the Southern, the great majority of the South Wales purchases coming straight from various BR storage locations at Salisbury, Weymouth, Eastleigh, Nine Elms and Redhill.

Positioned as they were, Kettering's main intake naturally consisted of 152 ex-LMS classes, the bulk of which were Black 5s, Stanier 8Fs and 4Fs. A large number of Jinties also ended their days here including No 47396 and other fellow shunters from Wolverton Works. Several of these arrived in 1967, including No 47482 which displayed its running number uniquely on the side tanks rather than cab. The only Eastern Region classes handled were B1s and the 2-8-0 heavy freight type O4.

Much rolling stock, including coaches and wagons surplus to BR requirements, was also handled as well as many of the local Oxfordshire and Northamptonshire ironstone locomotives in addition to other industrial motive power which took the one way ticket to Cohens.

The year 1965 was to be the peak time for arrivals from the Oxfordshire Ironstone Company, nine of their fleet, various Hudswell Clark, Peckett and Avonside saddle tanks all disappearing into the Cransley site. BR Standard types dealt with here included three of the 75xxx Class 4s, and a quintet of 76xxx Class 4s including No 76036 which came all the way from Chester, its last allocation. There were also a few Class 3 2-6-2-tanks with a similar number of 9Fs. Cutting of ex BR locomotives was still going strong into 1969 with Black 5s Nos 44878, 45353, both withdrawn from Lostock Hall in July 1968, being worked upon the following March as were Nos 45134 and 44816.

Although Cohens continued to buy stock from BR in the diesel era, most diesels were scrapped by BR themselves, just a few major yards like Cohens, Booths and Slag Reduction taking any appreciable numbers and even then they were generally less than 100 apiece. A couple of grounded DMUs 56310 and Parcels Unit 55998 were still awaiting their fate at the Cransley site in March 1980, both having been withdrawn in 1972 and having spent at least five years dumped in the yard. Cohen's connection with the SR continued into the post-steam age as No 74006, formerly E5023, withdrawn from Eastleigh in June 1976 due to fire damage, was noted in the yard in 1977. This was the only Class 74 to be broken up here. Previously Bulleid-Raworth electric locomotive No 20003 had arrived in the yard in 1969 from Durnsford Road, Wimbledon. Among the numerous diesel disposals were D5088 of Class 24, a number of WR Hymeks, no less than 13 D82xx types, No D8405, a Baby Deltic, and variety of shunters together with ex-Army locomotive WD843.

Cohen's other scrapping locations across the UK witnessed some notable departures including A4 No 60002 "Sir Murrough Wilson", which arrived at their Cargo Fleet site in October 1964 directly from store at Heaton MPD. Their operation at Tinsley Sheffield first came to notice in September 1962 when J26 No 65773 was spotted in pieces in the yard, although it is believed that this locomotive may have arrived semi-cut from Darlington Works. During the next five years other locomotives arrived here, never in appreciable numbers, whilst they also tended to be of the smaller types, such as LMS 4F, 2F, 1F and 0F classes. These included Nos 47002 / 47008 / 47009, 0-4-0STs and No 47164, a Fowler 2F Dock Tank. Perhaps their most notable victim was named B1 No 61249 "FitzHerbert Wright". The last locomotive recorded at Tinsley was 3F No 47534 in November 1967.

The Morriston Cohen's operation took no less than 98

ex-GWR types, mostly coming from local Welsh sheds, including eight Castles and 12 Halls. Mogul 5336, the last survivor of the series, also went to the Morriston site as did 29 Ivatt tanks including the ex-Somerset & Dorset examples. Occasionally parts were salvaged from locomotives and used to assist in restorations elsewhere as happened with Cransley's 8F No 48467, which in February 1969 carried on its side a message to the effect that spares would be taken to help in the restoration of sister locomotive No 48773 based on the Severn Valley Railway at Bridgnorth.

The Cransley site at Kettering is currently being redeveloped, thus it would seem that all traces of this fascinating location are likely to be lost in the future. Consequently only those haunting images of stock being reduced to scrap in bucolic surroundings often so very foreign to their former homes, will be there to remind us of the graveyard that once existed.

Top - W class 2-6-4T No 31914, one of four of the class scrapped at Cohen,s yard in rural Northamptonshire. (JG)

Bottom - Stovepipe-chimneyed No 30549 was the only member of Maunsell's Q Class to be scrapped at Kettering and it is seen here in company with a Q1 and more LT Underground stock.

12. Scrapping Factfile

FORMER SOUTHERN REGION STEAM LOCOMOTIVES BELIEVED TO HAVE BEEN SCRAPPED BY G COHEN OF KETTERING

Schools	30902 / 30921 / 30935
S15	30497 / 30507 / 30509 / 30514
H16	30518
Q	30549
Q1	33002 / 33008 / 33013 / 33016
W	31912 / 31914 / 31922 / 31924
Ivatt Tanks	41326 / 41327
Standard Class 4	76008
Standard Class 3	82011 / 82012 / 82013 / 82014 / 82015

REDHILL
N	31850

EASTLEIGH
MN	35004
U	31619 / 31809
N	31866
Q1	33015
St Cl 5	73041
St Cl 4	80132
USA	DS235 / DS236 (30066 / 30074)

PRIVATE SCRAPYARDS INVOLVED IN SCRAPPING SR LOCOMOTIVES FROM 1964 IN ORDER OF NUMBERS OF LOCOMOTIVES HANDLED

CONTRACTOR	LOCATION	TOTALS	
CASHMORE (87)	NEWPORT	15	N
		13	U
		5	S15
		5	Q1
		1	M7
		6	USA
		5	MN
		36	WC
		1	Z
BIRDS GROUP (45)	MORRISTON	18	N
		3	U
		9	Q1
		2	S15
		2	W
		1	MN
		10	WC
WOODHAMS (45**)	BARRY	9	S15
		1	Q
		1	N
		4	U
		10	MN
		20	WC

No 80132 being despatched by Cohen's "Flying Cutters" outside the front of the steam shed at Eastleigh. Just visible in the background is M7 No 30053, stored at the time pending a sojourn in the USA. (George Woods)

SCRAPPING FACTFILE

BUTTIGIEG (31)	NEWPORT	1 S15		WARD (5)	GRAYS	3 U
		1 U				2 Q
		2 N		WARD (5)	KILLAMARSH	5 Q
		2 Q1				
		6 MN		BR WORKS# (4)	EASTLEIGH	3 MN
		19 WC				1 WC
KINGS (20)	NORWICH	4 N		COHENS (3)	MORRISTON	2 N
		1 N1				1 Q
		3 U1				
		3 K		SLAG REDUCTION (3)	ROTHERHAM	1 U
		1 Q				2 MN
		7 Q1				
		1 H		WOODFIELD (2)	NEWPORT	1 MN
COHENS (17)	KETTERING	3 V				1 WC
		4 S15				
		1 Q		COX & DANKS (1)	PARK ROYAL	1 Q
		4 Q1				
		1 H16				
		4 W				

Post June 1964
** Only 4 of these locomotives were in fact scrapped.

SETTLE SPEAKMAN (16)	QUEENBOROUGH	2 S15	
		4 Q	
		4 M7	
		1 H	
		1 N	
		4 WC	

TOTALS BY CLASS

S 15	25
Q	18
Q1	29
N	48
N1	1
U	31
U1	3
M7	17
H	5
MN	30
WC	99
V	3
W	6
H16	1
Z	1
02	17
USA	8
K	3
GRAND TOTAL	**345**

WARD (15)	BRITON FERRY	12 M7
		3 H
SOLIFFE (11)	NEWPORT (IOW)	1 O2
BIRDS GROUP (8)	BYNEA	1 N
		4 U
		1 Q
		2 WC
COHENS FLYING SCRAPPERS (8)	EASTLEIGH	1 MN
		2 U
		1 N
		1 Q1
		2 USA
	REDHILL	1 N
HAYES (7)	BRIDGEND	6 WC
		1 Q
BIRDS GROUP (6)	RISCA	2 S15
		2 N
		1 Q1
		1 MN
BR WORKS (6)	RYDE I.O.W.	6 02

The above information is taken from the various "**What Happened to Steam**" publications by P B Hands and, as it is currently the subject of further study and correction under the banner "**What Really Happened to Steam**", the information should only taken as a guide. Initial reports suggest that there are not too many errors in the scrapping locations of SR locomotives. However, the dates given for scrapping are in some instances the dates of sale and not necessarily the actual dates of scrapping, which could be several months later and it would be misleading to accept them as such.

NB Thomas Ward of Ringwood cut four complete Standard locomotives plus a vast amount of scrap from Eastleigh which arrived by the wagonload eg. M7s 30034/30112, 30107 plus E4 32479. The complete locomotives which were cut here were 80096/80102 in March 1966 plus 75072/75073 from the S&D in April 1966.

It is known that scrapmen from Cashmore's in Newport travelled to Weymouth where, in January 1967, Standard No 73170 was cut up on site.

Top - No 34004 "Yeovil" seen at Southampton Central during the dying days of steam lasted in traffic until the very end - 9 July 1967. Middle - Remarkably, No 34004 retained its crest, scroll and nameplate well into the final year.

Bottom - A lifetime of service ends on the scrapline at Weymouth, the tender, now containing the connecting rods, being suitably inscribed "Well Done SR's Good and Faithful Servant R.I.P.". It is also easy to see how bridge strikes occurred with the roads positioned as such. (All JG)